## Praise for *How the Hell Did This Happen?*

"Where are we going? Where have we been? P. J. O'Rourke casts his gimlet gaze on the circus of clowns-people foisted on us by the 2016 election—and demands to know *How the Hell Did This Happen?*"                —*Vanity Fair*

"O'Rourke has a real eye for the vagaries of American politics."                —*Guardian* (UK)

"Entertaining as O'Rourke's quips generally are, it's when he gets to the heart of the matter, discussing the mob mentality and the value of 'individual dignity, individual freedom, and individual responsibility,' that his work is most pointed."                —*Publishers Weekly*

## Praise for P. J. O'Rourke

"The funniest writer in America."    —*Wall Street Journal*

"P. J. O'Rourke is like S. J. Perelman on acid."
—Chris Buckley

"[P. J. O'Rourke] was really the first to inject non-liberal hilarity into political discourse . . . But more important, he was able to yank conservatives out of the hands of the humorless and shrill, and make such writing accessible . . . He changed my life."        —Greg Gutfeld

"Whether you agree with him or not, P.J. writes a helluva piece."                —Richard Nixon

# How the Hell Did This Happen?

## A Cautionary Tale of American Democracy

# P. J. O'Rourke

Grove Press UK

First published in the United States of America in 2017
by Grove/Atlantic Inc.

First published in Great Britain in 2017 by Grove Press UK,
an imprint of Grove/Atlantic Inc.

This paperback edition published in 2018

A CIP record for this book is available from the British Library.

Paperback ISBN 978 1 61185 511 1
E-book ISBN 978 1 61185 951 5

Printed in Great Britain by Clays Ltd, St Ives plc

Grove Press, UK
Ormond House
26–27 Boswell Street
London
WC1N 3JZ

www.groveatlantic.com

To Morgan Entrekin
My editor, my publisher, and, best of all, my friend

"A pity they both can't lose."

—comment on the Iran-Iraq War
attributed to Henry Kissinger

# CONTENTS

# AUTHOR'S NOTE

I knew that the months leading up to the 2016 presidential election would be interesting times. I had no idea they would rise to the level of an ancient Chinese curse.

There isn't, incidentally, any such thing as an ancient Chinese curse saying, "May you live in interesting times." The phrase seems to be a piece of invented Orientalist folklore coined in the 1930s by First Lord of the Admiralty Sir Austen Chamberlain, half-brother of Prime Minister Neville Chamberlain who went off to Munich to appease Hitler. And let's not be silly and forget that the Chamberlain brothers lived in much more accursedly interesting times than our own.

What I *thought* was going on in the 2016 election cycle was a mere fight to the death between two fundamental American political ideologies.

The inevitable, inexorable, predestined Democratic candidate, Hillary Clinton, was an embodiment of liberal orthodoxy as it has been handed down from on high for eighty-four years, since FDR's election in 1932.

Clinton was an ancient monument of liberalism. If Washington were Pharaonic Egypt—and sometimes it is—Hillary would be the Sphinx. With the exception that she never shuts up. And she's hardly immobile. For the past quarter of a century she's been everywhere we looked.

So there was the monumental Hillary out in the American electoral desert surrounded by a Republican horde of . . . of whatever small, feckless, puny fauna Egypt has. I've Googled the matter. Yes, there it is exactly—"Giza gerbils."

These were the forces of the resurgent American conservatism that began its rise with the election of Ronald Reagan and then quit rising and started to droop into simplistic Tea Party obstructionism.

However, the outcome of the battle was not a foregone conclusion. Even a gerbil might be able to outsmart something with a head full of rocks.

And the Obama Administration, which was supposed to be the Great Pyramid of Cheops, had turned out to be a somewhat aimless enterprise. Not that it didn't take aim at a lot of things, letting feeble, sanctimonious darts fly in every direction that right-minded people could think of. But only one arrow sank home—a perhaps well-meaning but ridiculously complex and dubiously viable healthcare reform. And the president had just barely managed to avoid standing fully in the way of an overdue economic recovery.

If Hillary won, liberalism would become a permanent feature of the American landscape, like the Rocky Mountains but more expensive to ascend.

If a Republican won, conservatism would flow freely again, a mighty Mississippi of entrepreneurial initiative and individual responsibility with a lot of muddy corruption at the bottom.

Meanwhile, the American public wasn't holding either political party in much esteem. What the American public was holding was its nose.

Therefore I was prepared for some surprises during the 2016 campaign, which leaves me with no excuse for how surprised I was by what the surprises were.

Most of the chapters in this book were written while the events described were taking place. Reading the manuscript I notice there's a lack of continuity between the chapters. One thing doesn't lead to another. This is because, in the 2016 presidential campaign, as far as I can tell, one thing *didn't* lead to another.

The campaign was a series of singularities. Little universes kept expanding out of nothing and disappearing into space. It was as if God were letting some of the junior angels, Cherubim perhaps, take practice shots with the Big Bang. I would have preferred to write a book about the course of actions taken during this election campaign and how that course of actions led to certain results. But there was no discernable course. The course might as well have been at Trump University. And the results might as well have been determined by a pair of twelve-sided dice used by stoned Bernie Sanders supporters in a game of Dungeons & Dragons. (*Dungeons & Dragons* being a not-bad alternative title for what you hold in your hands.) Anyway, if my book lacks a coherent narrative it's because I couldn't find one.

We also don't yet know what the outcome of this election means. We may not know for years. If the outcome of the election means the end of the world, as my liberal friends seem to think, we'll never know. In that case we'd better have fun while we can. And, despite the random nature of the campaign and the opaque nature of its consequences, the thing was undeniably fun to write about.

It is my hope that it will be fun to read about too, and, maybe, produce the corner of a smile with which to catch a teardrop. Furthermore, now's the time to do the writing and the reading, before we forget all about the minor characters who provided such splendid comic relief in this drama, such as Governor John . . . John . . . Begins with a K . . . It's on the tip of my tongue . . . Oops, too late.

P. J. O'Rourke
*Christmas, 2016*
*March Hare Farm*
*New Hampshire*

# PREAMBLE ,

We the people of the United States, in order to dissolve what unity we have, establish injustice, insure domestic idiocy, provide for the common offence, promote the general despair, and secure enmity toward ourselves by our posterity, do ordain and establish this obnoxious political spectacle, the election of 2016.

# I
# The Campaign Begins

*Ready, Set, Go to Hell*

Who are these jacklegs, highbinders, wire-pullers, mountebanks, swellheads, buncombe spigots, boodle artists, four-flushers, and animated spittoons offering themselves as worthy of the nation's highest office?

Do they take us voters for fools?

Of course they do. But are they also deluded? Are they also insane? Are they receiving radio broadcasts on their dental fillings telling them they have what it takes to be a good president?

Perry, Santorum, Walker, Webb, Chafee, Pataki, Huckabee, Jindal, Graham, O'Malley, Paul, Fiorina, Biden, Bush, Christie, Carson, Rubio, Cruz, Kasich, Sanders, Clinton, and Trump.

That's not a list of presidential candidates. That's the worst law firm in the world. That's a law firm that couldn't get Caitlyn Jenner off on a charge of Bruce Jenner identity theft.

These people don't even have what it takes to be a bad president.

Show me one candidate who, like Millard Fillmore in 1856, has the honest decency to come right out and admit being a "Know-Nothing."

At least the members of the Know-Nothing Party knew they knew nothing.

Or show me one candidate who says nothing. Calvin Coolidge had nothing to say and, in his outspoken manner, said it.

Failing that, show me one candidate who can be counted on to keel over dead thirty-two days after inauguration the way William Henry Harrison did.

The 2016 candidates do not possess William Henry Harrison's kind of gravitas. (Although Chris Christie does possess William Howard Taft's kind of *gravity*.)

And the candidates aren't lighthearted. None has grown sideburns as amusing as Chester A. Arthur's. Nor—so far as we know—spends evenings in frolic with as plump and giddy an intern as Monica Lewinsky.

Even the nuts among the 2016 candidates do not rise to the level of the nuts of yore.

Progressive Republican senator from Wisconsin Robert M. La Follette stood almost alone in his crusade to keep America out of World War I, pointing out that the issue of unrestricted German U-boat warfare had been resolved peacefully in Lake Michigan.

Presidential nominee William Jennings Bryan thundered to the Democratic National Convention of 1896, "You shall not crucify mankind upon a cross of gold." (One can hardly disagree. Although it sounds like an expensive idea and not very practical, and I don't believe anyone had actually proposed it.)

The array of 2016 presidential candidates raises two questions. Has the office of the presidency diminished in stature until it attracts only the leprechauns of public life? Or have our politicians shrunk until none of them can pass the carnival test "You Must Be Taller Than the Clown to Run for President"?

At the start of the 2016 presidential campaign (less than a minute after the finish of the 2012 presidential campaign) the outcome was foretold. The opinion was universally held, by the sort of people who universally hold opinions, that Hillary Clinton and Jeb Bush would be the inevitable winners of their parties' nominations.

And I trembled for my country.

Members of the electorate would go into the ballot booth, see the two names, "Clinton" and "Bush," and think to themselves, "Gosh, I'm getting forgetful. I *did* this already." They'd leave without marking the ballot. Voter turnout would be 6 percent.

The shuttle from the local old-age home would send a few senile Republicans to the polls. A Democratic National Committee bus would collect some derelicts from skid row. And we would have the first president of the United States elected by a franchise *limited* to sufferers from Alzheimer's disease and drunken bums.

What happened to Jeb Bush? He had everything. He's young (for a Republican), a Phi Beta Kappa, and a successful businessman. And he'd been a two-term governor of Florida, where balloting incompetence and corruption are vital to the GOP.

Jeb is fluent in Spanish. His wife is Hispanic. He's got a bunch of kids and they're Hispanic too. Maybe he'd choose Marco Rubio as his running mate. Kiss the Latino vote good-bye, Democrats.

Plus Jeb was rolling like a dirty dog in campaign contributions.

Yes, Jeb *Bush* did have one problem. We political pundits were slow to grasp it. Political pundits are under professional obligation to regard the obvious as being too obvious. If it were the job of political pundits to state the obvious, there—obviously—wouldn't be any need for political pundits. However, even we pundits were able to take a "Bush-league" guess at what Jeb Bush's problem was.

Yet we continued to believe Jeb would get the nomination right up until he placed fourth in a three-man race in the New Hampshire primary and shortly thereafter suspended his campaign with a total of four pledged delegates.

Even then I kept predicting he would win. I said, "Don't worry, Jeb is all set to legally change his name to 'George Herbert Walker Bush.' Everybody likes *him*. And he served only one term so he's constitutionally eligible to run again."

Meanwhile, Hillary Rodham Clinton maintained her position as the person the Democrats most wanted to nominate for president. Unless someone—*anyone*—could be found to replace her.

Hillary had an iron grip on second place. Whoever was ahead of her was so far ahead nobody knew who it was yet.

It is to be remembered that at this point in the 2008 election cycle, Barack Hussein Obama was about as likely to be nominated for president as some small-time community-organizing junior senator from Illi-wherever with a name like a man who tried to sabotage an airplane with an underpants bomb.

Speaking of airplanes, Hillary carries more baggage than the Boeing she used as secretary of state visiting every country in the world that later blew up in her face in her quest to fulfill the mission of the U.S. secretary of state, which is to accumulate frequent-flier miles.

She had Julian Assange set up her State Department e-mail server. She put the Dalai Lama on security duty at the U.S. consulate in Benghazi. The geopolitical conflicts of interest at the Clinton Foundation were so large they had to be weighed on Chris Christie's bathroom scale. And at any moment her horn-dog husband might slip his leash and get up to old tricks chasing nubile squirrels.

On the upside, Hillary *is* familiar with the White House—knows where the extra toilet paper is stored and where the spare key to the nuke missile launch briefcase is hidden (Truman Balcony, second pillar from the right).


Maybe the candidate who was ahead of Hillary was Joe Biden. Biden is a savvy guy. Biden once gave what is probably the most insightful and accurate assessment ever of Hillary's talents and abilities. He told a September 2008 Democratic campaign rally in Nashua, New Hampshire, "Hillary Clinton is as qualified or more qualified than I am to be vice president of the United States of America."

In 2016, however, we already had a vice president and, unfortunately for Joe, he was Joe. Thus Joe lost his edge facing someone who was as qualified as or more qualified than he was to be him.

Maybe the candidate ahead of Hillary was Senator Elizabeth Warren of Massachusetts.

Warren has Native American ancestry.

How.

As well you may ask. But it would be a fund-raising plus—if she got her own casino.

Warren is an expert in bankruptcy law; this gives her a vision for our nation's future.

She masterminded the Consumer Financial Protection Bureau. It's working. You can tell it's working by the 7 million student loans that are currently in default. Students would probably be making some loan payments if they didn't feel so well protected by the Consumer Financial Protection Bureau.

And Elizabeth Warren turned left—the only direction that GPS units give in the hybrid cars that vegan aroma therapist Democratic primary voters drive.


But, in fact, the candidate who was so far ahead of Hillary that we didn't know who it was yet was the screwy-kablooey commander of the Vermont-Cong, Senator Bernie Sanders.

Bernie says he wants to make America more like Europe.

Great idea! Europe has had a swell track record for a hundred years now—ever since Archduke Ferdinand's car got a flat in Sarajevo in 1914.

Make America more like Europe? Where do you even go to get all the Nazis and Commies and 90 million dead people it would take to make America more like Europe?

Bernie is a socialist. He says so himself. He thinks the Eighth Commandment, "Thou shalt not steal," doesn't apply to him, at least not when he's in public office. Bernie thinks our society should "share." He wants to take your flat-screen TV and give it to a family of pill addicts in the backwoods of Vermont.

Perhaps Bernie feels the same about the other nine Commandments. He and his supporters certainly don't have much use for the Tenth, "Thou shalt not covet thy neighbor's house, thou shalt not covet thy neighbor's wife, nor his manservant, nor his maidservant, nor his ox, nor his ass . . ." Especially if the ass in question is a Democratic Convention Hillary Super Delegate.

# 2
# The Abominable Showman

*June 16, 2015*

But then—from the bottom of the campaign barrel with the lees, dross, and dregs—came Donald Trump.

I have a campaign slogan for Trump; maybe it's a slogan for the entire 2016 presidential race, perhaps a slogan for all of America right now. It's a quotation from the English essayist and poet Charles Lamb.

Trump will need to Google "Charles Lamb." Trump has written eighteen books, leaving himself with little time to read any.

Charles Lamb said:

*If dirt was Trumps, what hands you would hold!*

The American government is of the people, by the people, for the people. And these days America is peopled by 320 million Donald Trumps. Donald Trump is representative of all that we hold dear: money. Or, rather, he is representative of greed for money. We common folk may not be able to match Trump's piggy bank, but even the most high-minded and charitable among us can match his piggishness.

The Clinton Foundation accepted a $500,000 donation from the government of Algeria.

To cite Amnesty International's 2014/2015 report on Algeria:

> *Women faced discrimination . . . and remained inadequately protected against violence. . . . Impunity prevailed for perpetrators of gross human rights abuses . . . and acts of torture.*

And the other thing that we hold dear is us. We, ourselves. In this era of the great and cherished self, admiration for which has become so fundamental to Americanism that self-esteem is taught in our schools, we can all match Trump's opinion of his own worth. Trump claims to be worth billions, seven of them as of 2012.

In 2004 *Forbes* magazine estimated Trump's net worth to be $2.6 billion. *New York Times* reporter Timothy O'Brien looked into the numbers and came up with a net worth figure between $150 million and $250 million. Trump sued O'Brien. Trump lost.

In June of this year Adam Davidson, a founder of NPR's show *Planet Money*, wrote an article in the *New York Times Magazine* with similar import.

Davidson notes that Trump is no longer even a minor player in the luxury resort and gambling business. He owns no casinos. Nor is he the principal owner of his own reality TV production company. Trump's Manhattan real-estate operation does not even rate a mention in the industry's "major rankings of developers, owners or property managers."

Trump's election filings showed $165 million in liquid assets. This makes him a rich man in my world but hardly a financial behemoth in the world where Trump claims to live. Davidson says, "His scattershot approach to branding might also hint at cash-flow issues."

"When you try to weigh Trump's record as a businessman," Davidson says, "you quickly find that there's nothing of substance. . . . His true calling seems to be acting like a successful businessman."

Many a political candidate has fibbed on the subject of his or her economic circumstances. For example, DOA President William Henry "born in a log cabin" Harrison. He was a former governor of Indiana Territory and a major Hoosier land speculator.

Or Hillary "dead broke" Clinton. Big shout-out to Algerian president-for-life Abdelaziz Bouteflika.

But Trump is the first candidate to—like the American legend that he is—tell tall tales about all the money he's got. Trump is a financial Davy Crockett, Johnny Appleseed, Paul Bunyan, and Babe the Blue Ox rolled into one, according to Trump.

If Trump's critics don't think this is typical of modern Americans, they haven't looked at our online dating profiles.

Also typical of modern Americans is Trump's bad taste. True, he doesn't dress the way the rest of us do— like nine-year-olds in twee T-shirts, bulbous shorts, boob shoes, and league-skunked sports team caps. And Trump doesn't weigh 300 pounds or have multiple piercings or visible ink. He puts his own individual stamp on gaucherie.

Trump's suits are expensive, according to Trump, but they have a cut and sheen as if they came from the trunk sale of a visiting Bombay tailor staying in a cheap hotel in Trump's native Queens and taking a nip between fittings. Trump wears neckties in Outer Borough colors. And, Donald, the end of your necktie belongs up around your belt buckle, not between your knees and your nuts. Trump's haircut makes Kim Jong Un laugh.

Americans appreciate bad taste or America wouldn't look the way America does. And the way America looks is due, in no small part, to buildings Trump built.

In the 1970s he ruined Grand Central Station's Commodore Hotel, turning it into a "Grand Hyatt." Built in 1919, the handsome neo–French Renaissance tower was covered by Trump with cheap glazing—a giant seventies smoked glass coffee table to snort cocaine off, except, Trump being a jerk, all its surfaces are vertical.

Then there is the brassy-déclassé Trump Tower with its horrible huge pleated facade threatening Fifth Avenue with a cacophony of sheet metal accordion music.

And Trump Taj Mahal casino in Atlantic City bears the same relation to the noble white mausoleum in Uttar Pradesh as a turd bears to a prize in a Cracker Jack box.

Trump's grandfather, a German immigrant, changed the family name from Drumpf to Trump. This was a mistake. We could have had Drumpf Tower, Drumpf Taj Mahal, Drumpf Plaza Hotel, and President of the United States Donald Drumpf.

Trump does have a certain Drumpfkopf understanding of the American economy. The average American household debt is now more than $225,000. The average American family's credit card debt is almost $16,000. Trump restructured $3.5 billion in business debt and $900 million in personal debt between 1991 and 1994. "Restructured" being the Trump way of saying he didn't pay it.

We Americans know a leader when we see one. We can assume that Trump will further America's economic growth the same way he's furthered his own—with bad debt, bad debt, bad debt, and more debt.

We love debt. Otherwise America's national debt wouldn't have gone from $15 billion in 1930 to $18 trillion today. With Trump in the Oval Office we'll be headed for . . .

I just asked WikiAnswers, "What comes after trillions?" There's a thing called a "quattuordecillion," which is $1,000,000,000,000,000,000,000,000,000,000,000, 000,000,000,000,000,000,000,000,000,000,000,000, 000,000,000,000,000.00.

But are all those zeros a reason not to vote for Donald Trump? No. We have to consider what kind of president he would make. What would his foreign policy be? What domestic priorities would he push?

This is what makes me a Trump supporter. I support Trump because of something the political satirist H. L. Mencken said. He said, "Democracy is the theory that the common people know what they want, and deserve to get it—good and hard."

Trump's chief domestic policy will be to be on TV. As president, Trump can be on TV all the time, 24/7. This might not be a bad thing. Just doing his hair in the makeup room during commercial breaks should keep him too busy to push other useless, expensive, and unworkable domestic policies the way some recent presidents have done. Obamacare. I'll name no names. And Trump can yell, "You're fired!" as much as he wants. It will make for a healthy turnover in Trump cabinet appointees such as Dennis Rodman, Larry King, and Vince McMahon.

Trump is under the illusion that he's thirty-five times richer than he is. He thinks childhood vaccination caused the movie *Rain Man*. He believes Obama was born to the queen of Sheba in Karjackistan and raised by Islamacist wolves in the remote forests of Harvard Law School. Vladimir Putin, Xi Jinping, Ayatollah Khamenei, ISIS, the Taliban, and Hamas will be paralyzed with fear. Trump is crazier than all the other candidates put together. Who knows what this lunatic will do?

What he'll do is build thousands of Trump casinos, Trump hotels, and Trump resorts in Moscow, Beijing, Tehran, Raqqah, Kandahar, and the Gaza Strip. Then all of them will go bankrupt the way Trump Taj Mahal, Trump Plaza Hotel, and Trump Entertainment Resorts did. He'll destroy the power of our foes, leaving Russia trying to palm off eastern Ukraine on angry bondholders and China auctioning distressed property in the Spratly Islands.

Hell, this might just work.

# 3
# The Horror! The Horror!

No it won't.

The best case that can be made for Donald Trump is that American politics has turned into an unmapped and pestilential watershed in the heart of darkness, so let's send Mr. Kurtz upriver.

To understand how the heretofore more or less respectable Republican Party wound up with such a repellent nominee it's useful to look at the other prospective Republican nominees. And be repelled.

Almost the only two idiots the Republicans didn't consider nominating were Sarah Palin and Michele Bachmann—"Bullets and Booty." I was surprised they didn't gain stronger support. When was the last time the GOP had a smoking-hot electoral ticket? And, sure, Palin and Bachmann are nuts. But 42.9 million Americans over age eighteen suffer some form of mental illness. That's 30 percent of the popular vote.

*   *   *

Maybe Carly Fiorina could run America the way she ran
Hewlett-Packard. The way she ran Hewlett-Packard was
fabulous—if you shorted the stock.

Between July 1999 and February 2005, when Carly
was CEO, H-P's stock price fell 65 percent. I may forgive
Carly, but my Keogh plan never will.


Chris Christie had a certain appeal. In October 2014,
when Christie's Super Storm Sandy recovery plans were
questioned at a New Jersey town hall meeting, Christie
responded to the inquiring citizen by saying, "SIT DOWN
AND SHUT UP."

Some political pundits claimed that Christie's abra-
sive style wouldn't play west of the Jersey Shore. These
pundits were raised by pot-smoking parents and went
to Montessori schools.

"Sit down and shut up" is how all important family discussions begin and end everywhere in America.
America's family of voters applauds such concise state-
ments of foreign and domestic policy goals.

Then Christie got stuck in traffic.


Nonetheless I thought the guy might make a campaign
comeback. I mean, "SIT DOWN AND SHUT UP" was a
much livelier campaign slogan than any other presidential
candidate had.

Compare:

Bernie Sanders—*A Political Revolution Is Coming.* (Don't cross on the red.)

Jeb Bush—*Jeb!* (Interesting use of punctuation. Let's try it with various other punctuation marks. *Jeb . . . "Jeb" Jeb? Jeb**)

Rick Perry—*We Must Do Right and Risk the Consequences.* ("Truth or Dare!"—take your clothes off, Rick.)

John Kasich—*Kasich for Us.* (Interesting use of pronoun. Let's try it with various other pronouns. *Kasich for You, Kasich for Me, Kasich for Them, Kasich for It.*)

Martin O'Malley—*Rebuild the American Dream.*

Rick Santorum—*Restore the American Dream for Hardworking Families.*

Bobby Jindal—*Believe Again.*

Donald Trump—*Make America Great Again.*

(Why do they all want us to do everything twice? And by the way, Martin and Rick, rebuilding things in your sleep makes no sense at all.)

Rand Paul—*Defeat the Washington Machine. Unleash the American Dream.* (Somebody's been staying up late watching too many *Terminator* movies on Netflix.)

Ted Cruz—*Reigniting the Promise for America.* (Ka-boom.)

Lincoln Chafee—*Fresh Ideas for America.* (And organic and fair-traded and GMO-free.)

Jim Webb—*Leadership You Can Trust.* (To do what?)

---

* My brother was president and so was my dad!

**Carly Fiorina**—*New Possibilities. Real Leadership.* (As opposed to leadership you can trust.)

**Lindsey Graham**—*Ready to Be Commander-in-Chief on Day One.* (There are, however, 364 other days in a year.)

**Dr. Ben Carson**—*Heal. Inspire. Revive.* (If your insurance covers it.)

**George Pataki**—*People over Politics.* (Voters over easy.)

**Marco Rubio**—*A New American Century.* (Somebody's sixteen years late to the party.)

**Scott Walker**—*Reform. Growth. Safety.* (Is this a random word-association test? "School." "I don't like the look of that mole." "Adult diapers.")

**Mike Huckabee**—*From Hope to Higher Ground.* (Fine, if you're running for Mayor of New Orleans.)

**Hillary Clinton**—*Hillary for America.*

**Jim Gilmore**—*Gilmore for America.*

**Me**—*Beer for Breakfast.*

# 4
# A Huck So Unlike Finn

*July 26, 2015*

It would be completely unfair—and thus entirely in the spirit of this campaign—to single out one Republican candidate as an example of Republican candidates being so intellectually soiled that they lost the nomination to crap itself.

As an example, Mike Huckabee will do.

"Playing the Hitler card" is an infallible sign that a politician has run out of intelligent, substantive, and plausible ways to criticize an opponent. This would be amusing (Mel Brooks made Hitler amusing), except "playing the Hitler card" is also an infallible sign that a politician has run out of *amusing* ways to criticize an opponent.

Claiming, as Huckabee did on July 26, that the president of the United States "will take the Israelis and march them to the door of the oven" is not a cogent critique of the Iran nuclear deal however bad the deal is. Nor is it an insightful thing to say about the administration that made the bad deal.

And, Mike, it is not a Christian thing to say about Barack Obama. Perhaps you're one of those people who think the president isn't a Christian. That doesn't let you off the hook. John 10:16, "And other sheep I have, which are not of this fold." *Verbum Domini. Deo gratias.*

I'm a Christian too, Mike. Maybe I'm not a hard-shell Baptist ordained minister dog-in-the-manger-at-Bethlehem Christian like you are. But I think you could use a refresher course in Christianity.

Matthew 5:22, "Whosoever shall say to his brother, Raca, shall be in danger of the council." *Raca* is Aramaic for "fool." Council, in this case, means "group of people called together for consultation, discussion, advice." The group of people is decent, sensible Republican voters, and *raca* is what they think you are for playing the Hitler card.

And it's not just your "march them to the oven" comment that makes me think you need a come-to-Jesus moment.

I believe the Bible is the word of God. And you believe in creationism. "God created man in his *own* image," says Genesis 1:27.

Mike, look in the mirror. God is obviously telling you to lay off the biblical literalism.

You're a smart man. You graduated magna cum laude from Ouachita Baptist University, which has a "Department of Worship Arts." I doubt it includes any bowing down to the golden calf of secular humanism the way Hillary did at Wellesley.

So, Mike, you know about God. Do you think God is smarter than we are?

I'm a kind of god to my dog. When I say to my dog, "It shall be an abomination unto you to nose open the trash cabinet under the kitchen sink and eat garbage," what does my dog hear? *"Garbage!"*

Maybe you should consult I Samuel 18, verses 1 through 4: ". . . the soul of Jonathan was knit with the soul of David. . . . Then Jonathan and David made a covenant. . . . And Jonathan stripped himself of the robe that was upon him." And here you are trying to get in between them.

Mike, you're against gay marriage and gay adoption. Once people get married and have kids they don't have the energy for *any* kind of sex. They're parents. And when people become parents they turn into, pollsters tell us, *Republicans.*

Having you trying to convince people to vote for the GOP is like having Mahatma Gandhi on U.S. Marine Corps recruiting posters.

You call for "civil disobedience" to halt gay marriage. And you compare this to the actions of Gandhi and Martin Luther King. Mahatma and MLK would walk down the street in assless chaps at the Gay Pride Parade before they'd join you in a sit-in.

And you don't like immigrants coming to America and making money. When people come to America and make money, what do they turn into? Again, *Republicans.*

You want 10 million illegal immigrants to return to their countries of origin within 120 days. Otherwise they'll be banned from coming to America, *where they already are.*

Lights on in your head, Mike.

You say displaying the Confederate battle flag is "not an issue" for a presidential candidate. Not an issue, if you don't want any black person to ever vote Republican in this or any other dimension of the universe from now until end-time. You'll have Clarence Thomas putting up Bernie Sanders yard signs if you don't stop talking smack.

Mike, my Republican friends would rather hoist the Jolly Roger than fly the rebel flag like a bunch of cement-head biker trash with swastika face tattoos.

At least pirates believe in free enterprise, which, by definition, doesn't include human bondage—unless it's the kind people pay to stream on their laptops. George Washington Carver did not have a "safe word."

Mike, to what political party do you think Abraham Lincoln belonged? We *won* the Civil War.

And my Republican friends aren't distressed about LGBT rights or undocumented aliens. Who do you think decorates Republicans' houses? The guys from the Moose Lodge? And who mows Republicans' lawns? Lincoln Chafee?

You're non compos mentis, Mike. You were on John McCain's short list for running mates and he picked Sarah Palin for her comparative sanity.

Furthermore, Mike, as a hard-shell Baptist, you are accused of teetotaling until proved innocent. I don't want any damn sweet tea in my stemware when you invite me to a state dinner at the White House. And you may have to. I'm the only inside-the-Beltway type who'd come.

Because you wrote a book called, *God, Guns, Grits, and Gravy*. It's a great title and—what with the saying of grace, the Glock I'm cleaning, and the pork ribs and collard greens—that's pretty much what's on my table.

"Marriage as an institution is not so much threatened by same-sex couples as it is by heterosexuals' increasing indifference to it." That's *you* in *your* book. Maybe you should reread *GGG&G* as well as the Bible.

Mike, you think God is involved in politics. Observe politics in America. Observe politics around the world. Observe politics down through history. Does it *look* like God is involved? No. That would be the "Other Fellow" who's the political activist.

No, your candidacy won't disappear instantly—not until the Holy Roly-Polies, snake handlers, Rapture chasers, and flat-earthers have met at their Iowa caucus tent revivals and borne witness to your divinely inspired campaign.

Then, however, as is foretold in Revelation 22:15, you will look around at the field of other candidates and realize that "without are dogs, and sorcerers, and whoremongers, and murderers, and idolaters" and you'll go back to Fox News and AM talk radio.

But even there you aren't the "In-the-beginning-there-was-the-Word" that you once were, Mike. National opinion is flowing so fast against your brand of conservatism that you look—even to God-fearing Republicans—like a fat man trying to row up Class 5 rapids on a standing paddleboard.

Yes, you have your base. There are the no-account gospel-grinding, pulpit-hugging evangel-hicks who think that the answer to every question including "What to wear to the prom?" is found in Leviticus, chapters 17 to 26, in English like what God spoke to Moses.

But, as I said, it's the "Other Fellow" who's involved in politics. And he will reap what you've helped to sow.

*For, behold, the day cometh, that shall burn as an oven: and all the proud, yea, and all that do wickedly, shall be stubble.*

—Malachi 4:1

# 5
# Always Look on the Bright Side of Life

So far I have been striking a rather sour note in this book. Readers are hopeful people. Otherwise—given how little hope there is that the outcome of this election will be other than disastrous for the kind of people who can read—they wouldn't be reading about it. Hopeful readers are saying to themselves, "Surely there was *something* good about the 2016 presidential campaign. Certainly there was at least one candidate who wasn't a complete jerk."

Well . . .

In September 2014, when a faint glow of promise and expectation could still be discerned upon this election's distant horizon, I did have a talk with Rand Paul.

The office of Senator Paul, advocate of limited government, is in the Russell Senate Office Building—limitlessly huge, forbidding, and labyrinthine to the extent that I got lost three times trying to find him.

Senators and their staffers used to fit into the Capitol building, which is, you'd think, huge enough for any 100 dignitaries. But according to the Senate Historical

Office website, "With the steady growth of legislative business . . . Congress has constantly struggled to create sufficient workspace."

Construction of the Russell Building began in 1906 during the "Progressive" era. Until 1972 it was called simply the Senate Office Building—SOB for short. Then the SOB was named for one, Senator Richard Russell, who represented Georgia from 1933 until 1971 and was notable mostly for his support of segregation.

I said to Senator Paul, "I don't know if what I need is an interview or a sociopolitical therapy session. Libertarian political principles must be applicable to practical politics or what are political principles for? But, what with the Russell Building and all, I'm not feeling it. I'm deeply conflicted. Although I know you're not that kind of doctor."

"I could do an exorcism," Senator Paul said.

He described his own political situation, "If I try to be a pretty good libertarian I get attacked by the left, by the right, and by the libertarians."

This was the same as General Ferdinand Foch's message to Marshal Joseph Joffre during the First Battle of the Marne—"My center is giving way, my right is retreating, situation excellent, I am attacking"—except in this case not in French and said with a smile.

As for political principles, Senator Paul said, "In Washington principled individuals are in the minority. There's a good side to this. The majority can be influenced by public opinion."

And, reversing Lord Acton's maxim about power corrupting, Senator Paul thinks the lack of it purifies: "As opponents to President Obama we're more principled than when we were in power."

(I hoped, at the time, that Senator Paul was right about this. Subsequent Republican behavior did not, however, prove his thesis.)

"A principled GOP could," said the senator, "find people on both left and right to cooperate on issues." He listed some:

"The inequities of the criminal justice system."

"Government surveillance."

"Fourth Amendment privacy."

The Fourth being the amendment about how people have the right to be secure in their persons, houses, and papers—which should prohibit the government from poking around in my iPhone looking for sexts. I'm pushing seventy. I don't know how to text, and I don't remember much about sex either.

"The economy," Senator Paul said. "Although that's mostly on the right. But some on the left are beginning to realize what's wrong, sort of."

"Foreign policy," he added.

I wasn't going to bring that up. Senator Paul had been getting a dunking in the media for his flip-flops on foreign policy. To my mind this was nothing compared with the flip-flops done by foreigners. (Foreigners being something foreign policy, alas, has to take into account.) NATO ally Turkey had flipped—opposing us against ISIS. (The Turks later flipped back.) Iran had flopped—opposing ISIS against us. Assad, the Syrians who hate him, and Iraqi Sunni tribesmen were all flipping and flopping. Our foreign policy canoe was filled to the gunwales with catch-and-release terror trout armed with AK-47s. I'm not surprised a senator—or even a president—had to change his mind about which of these fishy characters to whack on the head with the paddle.

Senator Paul didn't mention his critics but said, "Congress *does* have a say." And he went on to give as much of a *Rand Paul Middle East Doctrine* as a place where doctrine is the problem can take.

"The fighting needs to be done by the people who live there. They all recognize barbarity. The Kurds are worth helping. We know what they want. They know what they want. They're fighting to get it."

"What are the Iraqis fighting—or not fighting—for?" I asked.

The senator thought the only way to get the Iraqis' allegiance was to pay for it. Not that he thought the Iraqis could be bought. "They need to be re-rented," he said.

Senator Paul pointed out a cruel Middle Eastern irony. (The region has no other.) "Toppling secular dictators," he said, "has caused more trouble than anything else. Gadhafi hadn't been a threat for a long time. Saddam Hussein wasn't a threat. Assad isn't a threat. Egypt may be a little different. We didn't have very much to do with that."

I suppose, when America starts nation building, we'd better know what kind of Lego sets are available locally. Anyway, the nation Senator Paul would most like to build is America. And an important part of that project is cleaning up and putting away the vast number of interlocking government blocks of bureaucracy and pointy-headed figurines of officialdom scattered across our national carpet causing us to yell *Ouch!* and hop on one foot when we try to go anywhere without wearing our regulatory lawyer and tax accountant shoes.

Senator Paul said, "Any number of arguments for limited government can be made, but just two are necessary. First is the Thomas Paine natural liberty argument."

We surrender certain of our natural liberties to a government of our own making in return for public safety and order. Government is a necessary evil, and like all evils, however necessary, should be kept as small as possible.

My example would be servings of vegetables. Some varieties of kale grow to a height of six or seven feet. I don't want that on my dinner plate next to a T-bone steak the size of a Susan B. Anthony dollar.

"Second," said Senator Paul, "is the Milton Friedman efficiency argument."

In his 1980 PBS TV series *Free to Choose*, Friedman drew a simple graph showing that, mathematically, there are only four ways to spend money:

|  | Spent on You | Spent on Other People |
|---|---|---|
| Your Money | 1 | 2 |
| Other People's Money | 3 | 4 |

Spending your money on yourself is efficient. Tonight's special, prime rib with a *small* side dish of kale, looks like a good deal.

Spending your money on other people is efficient too. She'll have the mac and cheese.

Spending other people's money on yourself is not so efficient. The Wall Street Hedge Fund Managers' Association Annual Dinner will be at Maxim's in Paris.

But spending other people's money on other people— that is the way government spending is done. Free caviar for all Americans! Whether they like caviar or not. And get in line because there's nothing except caviar, and it will be rationed.

Senator Paul called himself "libertarianish," willing to vote against planks in the platform of the Libertarian Party. "Of which I am not a member."

There's a difficulty with the capital-L Libertarian Party. (Seats in the Senate 0. Seats in the House 0. Governorships 0. Seats in state legislatures 0.)

"The difficulty," said Senator Paul, "is that everyone has his or her opinion, and everyone knows he or she is right."

Libertarians are strictly logical so, it stands to reason, every libertarian is right. And everyone else, including every other libertarian, is wrong.

"Isn't that," I said, "an odd outcome for a political theory based on the value of each individual?"

The senator smiled and shrugged. "I never really felt like it was a problem explaining libertarian principles in practical politics. Republicans are champions of economic liberty. Democrats are champions of personal liberty. Bring the two back together."

The senator said, "The problem is mostly how people characterize libertarianism. But that's changing. Libertarian has gone from being something scary to something people like as a label for themselves."

He said, "There are different ways to get where we want to go." And gave an example of going nowhere. "Nothing good has come out of the war on drugs."

"What's a different way?" I asked.

"I like the unenumerated powers."

*The powers not delegated to the United States by the Constitution, nor prohibited by it to the states, are reserved to the states respectively, or to the people.* The tenth right in the Bill of Rights keeps us from having just nine rights.

"In *The Federalist Papers*," I said, "Hamilton argued *against* the Bill of Rights on the grounds that when government even so much as mentions rights like free speech this implies that government has some power over those rights."

"But it's a good thing we did write them down," the senator said, "otherwise we'd have *nothing* left."

Senator Paul asked, not quite rhetorically, "Is this the 'libertarian moment'? If so, it probably won't come from a third party. Probably it will come from within a party."

"From within the Democratic Party?"

He didn't seem to think it was inconceivable. "In New Hampshire," he said, "even Democrats are against state income and sales taxes."

But he didn't seem to think it was likely either. "Republicans are an ideological coalition," he said. "Democrats are a coalition of ideologies. The only thing Democrats agree on is income redistribution."

Senator Paul said, "Republicans have tradition on their side. It's the American Revolution versus the French Revolution."

This was a switch—a flip-flop if you will—from Thomas Paine's radical liberty de facto to Edmund Burke's traditional liberty de jure. But I don't fault the senator. No friend of liberty can avoid the tumble back and forth between Burke and Paine.

"Tradition is a good thing," the senator said. "Ninety percent of Americans don't break the law, not because there's a law against it, but because they have a tradition of conscience. Republicans are traditional. But tradition can be boring. Libertarianism spices things up. Republicans have to either adapt, evolve, or die. They either have to water down their message—or extend liberty."

I walked back to my hotel in a cheerful mood. And the longer the mood lasted the more it alarmed me. Did I want an exorcism? I'd been politically engaged, as they call it, for fifty years—since I went with high school friends to picket Barry Goldwater for fear he'd get us into a war in Southeast Asia or something. In the meantime I'd been disappointed by twenty-five Congresses and eight and a half presidencies.

A principled campaign for limited government. It's the thing with feathers. That perches in the soul. And craps on the liver? I tried to kick a pigeon. I walked into a gloomy bar.

# 6

# So Much for That

*A Pre-Postmortem Conducted on the Rand Paul Campaign*

To answer Senator Paul's question, "Is this the 'libertarian moment'?" No.

We were able to begin asking what went wrong with Rand Paul's presidential campaign before Rand Paul's presidential campaign began.

Let's start with the fact that I like him.

A journalist mustn't become fond of a candidate. Not because the journalist loses objectivity. What journalist even pretends to be objective these days? And not because of conflict of interest. Journalism is no longer of any interest.

Plus, when it came to conflict on the campaign trail, there wasn't much—at least not between those Republican primary candidates who were more or less in their right minds. They wound up in conflict for conflict's sake. It was like watching *The View*.

Journalists and candidates shouldn't be friends because journalism is the pig trough of American politics, and candidacy is the outhouse, and you, who read and vote, shouldn't be eating slop while you're sitting on the can.

I had a long phone conversation with Rand Paul in the summer of 2014 and, as reported in the previous chapter, I interviewed him that September.

It was a lousy interview. All Senator Paul and I did was enjoy a poli-sci geek yack about the strange reasoning behind Hamilton's *Federalist Paper* No. 84, the wonders of the Tenth Amendment, and our shared bafflement about why liberals and conservatives can't agree upon the Natural Rights they agree upon.

"No!" bark the conservatives; "John Locke said, 'life, liberty, and property'!" "No!" whine the liberals; "'life, liberty, and property' is what John Locke said."

I'm a lousy interviewer. Maybe I don't have the guts to ask the hard questions. Maybe I don't have the stomach to listen to the squishy answers. Or maybe I just don't have it.

The way Charlie Rose does.

**Charlie Rose:** Russia has intervened in Syria. What are Russia's intentions?

**Vladimir Putin:** Because you have guts to ask hard questions and earnest penetrating gaze meant to indicate high seriousness, I am compelled to tell you truth. We intend to nuke Kurds.

So, if you're looking for high-quality journalism giving the inside skinny on how the Rand Paul presidential campaign flopped, go watch *The View*.

But flop the campaign did. Among likely GOP voters, Rand polled somewhere between the number of holes left on the tongue of the belt on Chris Christie's pants and Kanye West. (I should quit making Chris Christie fat jokes. And I would, except, in the end, Christie comes out supporting Trump and proves himself to be *all* fat, starting with his head.)

Nor was there much flap to this flop. Rand polled above 5 percent only during a brief period when the half-deaf grizzled coots who answer dinnertime phone calls from political pollsters still had him mixed up with Pat Paulsen.

Yes, Rand wasn't an ideal candidate. He doesn't ooze the sticky Venus flytrap empathy nectar of Bill Clinton or exude the lunatic energy of Bill's wife on her gerbil-in-the-wheel campaign.

Rand does not have Reagan's ability to simplify issues until camels slip through needle eyes the way food stamps slip through the grocery budgets of welfare queens and into the hands of Cadillac dealers.

Rand is boyish, but without the smooth, insinuating charm of a—Hey, where's my wife? Where's my wallet?—Kennedy. And Rand, being boyish, can't get away with just standing around looking like a grown-up in the manner of George H. W. Bush.

Rand is freighted with his father, who, per Rand's own description of libertarians, is so rigidly logical in his logicality as to sometimes defy logic. But who among us (except Jeb Bush) doesn't have an aging dad who's a bit of a crank? Not my teenage daughters, they inform me.

And Rand has been known to step in it when asked the "hard questions." So? Consider stinking huge piles of enormous Trump logo dimensions "it." Consider muck boots in Trump ego-size 17 EEE doing the stepping. Consider Trump. Why would a Rand fumble on "Wither the economy?" or "What's next in the Middle East?" even register on the political seismograph?

I agree with Rand politically, in general, usually, I guess. (Knowing how Rand Paul will handle an issue and where he'll go with it is not exactly like watching Brady-to-Gronkowski in a Patriots game.) But, putting that aside, I can't see how Rand was worse than the people (Republicans *and* Democrats) who did better than he did in the polls.

It's impossible to be worse than two of them—Donald Trump and Bernie Sanders, the Donald Trump for people who are still living in their parents' basements.

The competition wasn't Rand Paul's problem. His problem was the "libertarian moment in America." Not only wasn't it now, it wasn't ever, and it probably never will be.

Rand isn't a pure, capital-L Libertarian. He calls himself a "constitutional conservative," favors legal limits on abortion, tolerates but does not endorse gay marriage, is willing to entertain some notion of American international military intervention, and doesn't even support legalization of recreational marijuana.

Libertarians would pass a law against not supporting legalization of recreational marijuana, if libertarians believed in passing marijuana laws.

But Rand is as close to a libertarian as an American presidential candidate is likely to get. He firmly believes the federal government should obey the rule "Mind your own business and keep your hands to yourself." This is the *Bill and Hillary Clinton Principle*. Hillary, mind your own business. Bill, keep your hands to yourself.

But being even close-to-a-libertarian is too close for comfort in American politics. Whatever truths we hold to be self-evident, we self-evidently are not a libertarian country.

The libertarian moment in America certainly wasn't September 13, 1788, when the U.S. Constitution went into effect—Article I, Section 2, "Representatives . . . shall be apportioned by adding to the whole Number of free Persons . . . three-fifths of all other Persons."

If there's a libertarian moment in the future it won't be while liberals are in charge. The libertarian moment can't happen while we all fry and drown—collectively, as a community, because it takes a village, etc.—owing to the climate change that liberals insist upon.

If there's a libertarian moment in the future it won't be while conservatives are in charge. The libertarian moment can't happen during the conservative Christian Rapture when the faithful are being transported to heaven. This will leave too many Democrats behind to let libertarianism flourish.

And if there's a libertarian moment in the future it won't be while moderates are in charge. Because there are three basic tenets to libertarianism:

Liberty of the individual

Dignity of the individual

Responsibility of the individual

And everybody hates at least one of them.

This year everybody hated all of them. Liberty of the individual is under assault from those who'd insert "Keep your damn tired, your poor, your huddled masses" into Emma Lazarus's poem on the Statue of Liberty and also from those who'd make Pope Francis pass out free condoms at his Madison Square Garden Mass.

Dignity of the individual has been left for dead by Donald Trump.

And Responsibility of the individual is being trampled across the political spectrum—from the congressional bluenoses snatching our moral free agency to the White House Rudolph the Red-Nosed Reindeer stuffing our property rights down the government chimney.

What could Rand have done differently?

He might have been able to sell a kind of libertarianism to voters, if he'd simply pitched himself as being what we all like to think of ourselves as being—"social liberals and fiscal conservatives."

Maybe Rand should have said, "Being a social liberal and a fiscal conservative means wanting to get high and have sex while saving money."

And who does not?

But what Republican is going to admit that in public?

Republicans are still fighting the culture wars, dug in on the front lines and courageously blazing away, never mind that the enemy has declared victory and gone home to celebrate with legalized marijuana at a same-sex wedding reception.

Democrats are too busy trying to figure out a way to take all the money away from Republicans and give it to the government so that government can do all the work while Democrats go to the gym.

And pure, capital-L Libertarians are eating Bagel Bites and drinking Diet Pepsi Max in front of their computers, logged into unmoderated chat rooms arguing the finer shades of meaning in Ayn Rand's pronouncement, "The conservatives see man as a body freely roaming the earth . . . with an electronic computer inside his skull, controlled from Washington. The liberals see man as a soul freewheeling to the farthest reaches of the universe— but wearing chains from nose to toes when he crosses the street to buy a loaf of bread."

Meanwhile, Ayn, looking down from the heaven she didn't believe in, is saying, "Get a job."

# 7

# The Last Damn Republican Presidential Candidate Debate I'll Ever Watch

*August 6, 2015*

If this was meant to be a circus, all ten Flying Wallendas refused to walk the high wire, there were so many clowns that none of them could get out of the tiny car, and the elephants just stood around relieving themselves.

If this was meant to be informative, Savonarola was piling books on the "bonfire of vanities" in Florence, children were playing with matches in the Library of Alexandria, and Wikipedia crashed.

If this was meant to be theater of the absurd, it wasn't a patch on a high school drama club production of Ionesco's *Rhinoceros*.

The Republican candidates' debate should have been presented by World Wrestling Entertainment instead of

Fox News and Facebook. I'm amazed it wasn't. Donald Trump and WWE promoter Vince McMahon are pals and sometimes business partners. Trump has previously "competed" in a WrestleMania match with McMahon— "Hair vs. Hair," which Trump "won." Trump was inducted into the WWE Hall of Fame in 2013.

All the pieces were in place for a professional wrestling match with much greater meaning and import than what we saw on August 6.

And with a great pro wrestling story line! A nine-man Republican tag team dragging Donald Trump around the ring by his pompadour, assuming it's real. Assuming it's not, they could jam the wig down on the ref's eyes. They'd toss Trump over the ropes into the audience. Trump would be embraced by little old ladies who would then jump into the ring and swat the nine Republicans senseless with their handbags.

I would have watched that. But it never happened.

So, why *did* I watch the Fox News/Facebook Republican Presidential Primary Debate?

Why would *anyone* watch it? Unless he was drinking and had lost the channel changer? Which I was and did.

However, I had the good luck to view the program with my father-in-law—forward artillery observer in WWII, career FBI agent, and retired head of corporate security for a Fortune 500 company. A Republican everyman if ever there was one.

My father-in-law not firing his snub-nose .38 into the TV screen was an admirable example of GOP primary voter self-discipline and restraint. This gave me hope that Republican primary voters would be sufficiently self-disciplined and restrained to avoid the temptation to pull the trigger on the GOP by casting ballots for Trump.

On the other hand, my father-in-law is deaf and had just had a cataract operation. I can hear and see all too well. The only thing that kept me from unloading my duck gun at the Samsung was my wife, who had pocketed the key to the gun cabinet.

Meanwhile, I gather that what I heard and saw wasn't even the semi-maybe-important thing that happened on Debate Day. I didn't give the five p.m. Republican candidates' "Kiddie Table" debate a looky-loo. I'll go to the big top, but I won't be ballyhooed into the sideshow to see the Amazing Seven-Headed Creature from the Bottom of the Polling Lagoon.

According to my father-in-law, 6 million other viewers of *Clash of the Also-Rans*, and 83 percent of Twitter comments, Carly Fiorina took her half-dozen opponents and wiped the floor with them.

"That's a smart gal," my father-in-law said. "She's tough. She had the answers. She slammed that braggart Trump. Slammed Kerry for giving Iran the atom bomb. She'll take all those women's votes away from Hillary."

My father-in-law follows the stock market. He owns Hewlett-Packard stock. As mentioned, Hewlett-Packard stock tanked while Fiorina was CEO, and it's never recovered. My father-in-law giving props to Carly was another admirable example of GOP primary voter self-discipline and restraint.

Thus, filled with false hopes, I was thinking to myself that Suicide Blond Donald Trump (dyed by his own hand) had committed political hara-kiri by raising a solitary paw when the candidates were asked who among them would *not* promise to support the eventual Republican nominee.

I was thinking that Trump's poll numbers might look like a college basketball score now, but surely self-disciplined, restrained Republican primary voters would rather plaster their Buicks with "Lean Forward" bumper stickers than have another Ross-Perot-off-his-meds third-party candidate holding the White House door open for the Billary Bandits.

Gosh, was I wrong. Never listen to a pundit. Is there such a thing as "magnetic back-assward"? We pundits and commentators have had our compass needles pointed in that direction for the past eighteen months. Want a stock tip? I would have told you that Carly's debate performance was a clear sign to buy H-P. As of this writing, the stock has lost another $18.48 since its close on August 6, 2015.

But back to the main debate. The key thing about the debate was content, the message each candidate was trying to convey. Messages such as . . . Well, my father-in-law and I were pretty busy discussing how Hewlett-Packard's stock was ready for a dead cat bounce. ("Dead cat bounce" is a Wall Street analyst technical term, short for "Anything will bounce once if you drop it from high enough.") Also, we needed to refill our glasses with the special vitamin that makes Jeb Bush interesting. I guess it makes Jeb interesting. I seem to have been resting my eyes every time Jeb answered a question.

Then I was distracted by the Fox News panelists. Gosh, that Megyn Kelly is a handpicked peach. Bret Baier, I'm informed by my mother-in-law, is a hunk. (As she put it, "What a nice-looking young man.") And

Chris Wallace has the Cary Grant distingué thing going, making other men his age (me) look like late-career Wallace Beery. These three should start a Chippendales for political junkies.

Also distracting was Trump's coif. I'm not going there. Too many have gone there before, including, it would seem, a family of angry squirrels who use Clairol. So I won't delve into the subject—for fear of angry squirrels.

The angry squirrels scared the other candidates too. They didn't pile on Trump. Instead Chris Christie and Rand Paul had a tiff.

Christie wants government to snoop on our phones. This is not a vote-getter. Chris has the prosecutorial look of someone who'd inform spouses about cell phone records of calls to Monkey Bump Premium Escort Service.

Paul wants government not to snoop. Because Rand Paul is (sort of, as I've explained) a libertarian.

Almost 100 percent of Americans *act* like libertarians. Our free market has Rand's namesake Ayn looking like Diogenes asleep in his barrel. We've privatized the legal code from hedge fund derivative top to crack den bottom. We indulge in libertinage that would leave Tiberius blushing. Our individualism is so fulsome it fills Facebook, Twitter, Tumblr, and Snapchat and spills into real life. We drive eighty-five in school zones.

But only 11 percent of Americans *identify themselves* as libertarians.

This, Senator Paul, is what the Fifth Amendment is there for.

Paul was out. Christie was out. Trump was so far out he'd cracked his coxcombed head on Yankee Stadium's right field foul pole.

So now we were down to seven semi-sane Republicans. Or eight, if Carly Fiorina did indeed bounce when dropped.


I'm sure the Republican candidates' next eleven debates were very interesting. It's a shame that the seven or eight semi-sane Republicans didn't do so well against Bruno Sammartino, Dick the Bruiser, Killer Kowalski, Gorgeous George, "Nature Boy" Buddy Rogers, Fritz Von Erich, Haystack Calhoun, The Sheik, and Bobo Brazil. The Republicans just couldn't seem to figure out how to deal with the piledriver, the headscissors, the gorilla press, the Indian deathlock, the camel clutch, or the coco butt. Although they were all masters of the sleeper hold.

# 8
# Say It Ain't So, Joe

*Hello, Biden, and Good-Bye*
*October 21, 2015*

Joe, the Democrats don't want you. That's fine by me. I'm a Republican. I don't want you either. I'm happy you announced that you're not running for president. But, to quote the universally acknowledged definitive study of practical politics, which starred Marlon Brando and Al Pacino, "It's not personal. It's strictly business."

Personally, I think you're a great guy. I'm just scared that you, a Democrat, could get elected—by a wide electoral and popular vote margin.

So, Joe, you and I understand each other. What I don't understand is your fellow Democrats. I've seen what they were saying about you in the mainstream media. . . .

Let me pause for a moment in writing this well-informed and insightful item of political punditry and clear up something for the readers.

Political pundits like myself speak a different language, "Punditese." When a conservative political pundit says "mainstream media," that's Punditese for "ass-kissing pinko milksops." (The clever type of conservative political pundits sometimes employ a pun, "lamestream media.")

Likewise, when a liberal political pundit says "right-wing fringe talk radio," that's Punditese for "clear-eyed, sober assessment of the facts."

A complete glossary of Punditese is contained in an appendix to this book.


As I was saying, Joe, it wasn't good. Your liberal pals in politics and the press were lining up to dump on you as if the organizers of "Campaign 2016" were threatening to take the porta potties away.

On September 2, CNN called you "a reliable fund-raiser for the Democratic Party." In Punditese, a bagman. And, to add slur to slander, they called you a "dutiful emissary of the administration's initiatives." Butt boy.

On August 28, in *Politico*, Katie Glueck wrote, "The vast majority of Democratic insiders . . . don't believe Joe Biden will run for president."

That's hardly an insult too bitter to swallow, since "political insiders" is a Punditese term for "I" or "me." But Ms. Glueck went on to cite *Politico*'s "weekly survey of the top strategists, activists and operatives in Iowa and New Hampshire" (which roughly translates as "people who bothered to answer my e-mails"). And a number of Iowa Cornball and New Hampshire Granite Pants anony-mous Dems unleashed derision and scorn upon you. For example:

"First and foremost, he is a loyal Democrat." (Transla-tion: "As was FDR's dog, Fala.")

"He's a truly wonderful man universally loved by NH Democrats." ("Like Jimmy Carter, but with a worse long-term political prognosis.")

"It's too late in the game for Biden to mount a serious bid." ("Biden's running? Nobody told me!")

"I have the utmost respect for him." ("Joe who?")

The *Atlantic*, the official journal of American *bien-pensants*, called you "another Beltway veteran" (i.e., liar, thief, and cheat). America's permissive libel laws notwithstanding, surely that's actionable.

And the *Atlantic* dragged out the twenty-seven-year-old supposed scandal about your plagiarizing a speech from British Labour Party leader Neil Kinnock—as if politicians write their own speeches.

Joe, you're a stand-up guy. It's not as though you believe in the same things as Edmund Burke (and me). But it's not as though Richard the Lionheart believed in the same things as Saladin. They were both stand-up guys. Your Democratic opponents are a couple of worthless little *sits*. One was a babysitter for two juvenile presidents, and the other is an Occupy Wall Street sit-in protester, except Vermonters didn't hate Wall Street enough to send him there so they put him in the Senate.

And, Joe, you've borne more personal sorrow than all the other presidential candidates, Democratic and Republican, combined. Borne it manfully.

Indeed, you've known more grief than all the other presidential candidates combined will give to the poor electorate over the next thirteen months. Which is a lot. And we Americans would be a happier people if you were in the race, even we Republican-Americans.

But you're not going to be.

The Big Donkeys want you kicked out of the Democratic candidate stable. They say you're "too prone to gaffs." The use of the Punditese loan word *gaff*, for which there is no exact English equivalent, makes it difficult to explain exactly what your fellow Democrats mean. But here are a few of your "gaffs" from a *Time* magazine online site called "Top 10 Joe Biden Gaffs."

You said about Obamacare on live TV, "This is a big fucking deal."

You told the House Democratic Caucus, "If we do everything right, if we do it with absolute certainty, there's still a 30 percent chance we're going to get it wrong."

And when you were running against Obama for the 2008 presidential nomination you described him as a "mainstream African-American who is articulate and bright and clean and a nice-looking guy." And said of his candidacy, "I mean, that's a storybook, man."

Perhaps the best I can do by way of explicating the nature of a "gaff" is to note that Punditese does not have a word for "truth."

But telling the truth is not your real problem, Joe. Your real problem is that you're an old, white European male. The Democrats are determined to elect "the first _____ American president."

African-American

Woman

Native American

Latino

Gay

They've checked off No. 1 and are determined to go down the list in order of historical victimhood.

Democrats are liberals, and—to their profound embarrassment—liberalism is an old, white European male political philosophy.

Liberalism is based on the thought of John Locke, Jean-Jacques Rousseau, Thomas Paine, and—oh, the shame of it—slave-owning, woman-exploiting Thomas Jefferson.

Liberalism is deeply confusing to liberals. America's first great liberal populist was Andrew Jackson, perpetrator of the genocidal Trail of Tears and annihilator of the Second Bank of the United States and hence of centralized economic control. (Sadly, Jackson put an end to the Second Bank of the United States before Hillary Clinton had a chance to claim large lecture fees for speaking to its executives.)

Plus, liberalism is painfully unhip. Say "Great Society" to today's with-it young Democratic voters and they hear air quotes around the "Great." LBJ is just another old, white European male. He was a warmonger. LBJ would have voted to invade Iraq like you, Joe, if he hadn't been an old, white, *dead* European male. FDR was a warmonger too. Say "New Deal" to millennials and they think you're talking about Texas Hold'em.

And now you say you aren't running. That's a shame, Joe. I hope it's not because you Googled yourself. (Google "Joe Biden quotes" and all the above-mentioned stuff comes up like a college binge drinking–flavored vodka barf.)

You were the Democrats' best choice, Joe. And not just because you're a decent, intelligent, and experienced man who is, by all accounts, cooperative with your political allies, respectful of your political opponents, and considerate to your staff.

Maybe, I thought, there was still hope. Read the next chapter, Joe, and I'll fill you in on why. I've been working on various plans for "A Better Way to Choose a President." Not that I consider myself a great political theorist. But, this year at least, I'd be hard pressed to come up with anything worse than the system we've got now. Tourists playing three-card monte on the streets of New York City have been doing a better job of picking a winner.

And, Joe, the good news for you is that under my best plan for a better way to choose a president—even though the plan is admittedly biased toward my own libertarian/constitutional conservative/is-it-cocktail-hour-yet? political leanings—you, Joe Biden, are leading in the polls.

# 9
# A Better Way to Choose a President, Part I

*Road Trip!*

By autumn of 2015 everybody in the United States except Donald Trump was thinking that there must be a better way to choose a president. And I believe I've got an idea that even Trump can accept.

Voters will ask themselves just one question: "Which candidate would I go on a road trip with?"

Trump, of course, imagines he'd win the Road Trip Poll—private jet! golf! luxury resorts! limos!

The rest of us are imagining spending an extended period of time in close quarters with the guy. How long would it be before I attached a hose to the exhaust pipe of the Lincoln Town Car and ran it into the passenger compartment? Or started chumming the water for sharks at Mar-a-Lago? Or drove a Titleist into the back of his skull from the second tee? Or got on the Darknet and began feeding ISIS information about my own flight plans with Donald on his 757?

One way or another, we'd be saying good-bye to Donald Trump.

Meanwhile, I've been researching the "Road Trip Poll." I've found that in the seventeen presidential elections held between 1948 and 2012, the R.T.P. selected the better candidate 70.5 percent of the time, which is 110 percent better than we're doing in this election.

I used the period after 1948 as the basis for my study because these are the optimal road trip years in American history.

By 1948 gas rationing had ceased, civilian auto production was in full swing, and plans for an "Interregional Highway" system were taking shape.

Before the 1940s a road trip was something the Joad family did in John Steinbeck's *The Grapes of Wrath*. Before that, America didn't have much in the way of roads. In 1919 the U.S. Army Motor Transport Corps drove a convoy of trucks from Washington, D.C., to San Francisco. It took fifty-six days. And before that, there were wagon trains.

In the movie *Animal House*, when a despairing Hoover asks, "What are we going to do?" Otter and Boon do not respond, "Westward migration of pioneer settlement!"


Consider the Road Trip Poll results:

> *Salty, poker-playing Harry Truman beginning each day with a shot of Old Grand-Dad* vs. *Thomas E. "little man on a wedding cake" Dewey*

Yes, Truman was a Democrat, which I am not. But he was honest about it. Dewey was a "progressive Republican."

This is a creature something like the pushmi-pullyu in the Dr. Dolittle stories except with two butt ends. (Nelson Rockefeller would become the progressive Republicans' other asshole.)

*Jolly golfer Ike* vs. *po-faced Adlai Stevenson*

Eisenhower won WWII. Stevenson was a special assistant to the secretary of the navy and in 1944 traveled to Italy as a representative of the U.S. Foreign Economic Administration to report on Italy's economy, which, in 1944, did not exist. Later he was the governor of Illinois for one term.

*Jolly golfer Ike* vs. *po-faced Adlai Stevenson rematch*

Even playing with a large handicap (1955 heart attack) Ike easily broke par. Adlai was in the rough for the rest of his life.

*Charming, charismatic JFK* vs. *Richard—no adjectives needed—Nixon*

A cinch for the R.T.P. Or so you'd think. A road trip with Richard Nixon would seem like gum surgery on wheels. But Hunter S. Thompson actually went on a road trip with Nixon—or, anyway, on a car ride—in New Hampshire during the 1968 presidential campaign. Hunter described it in *Fear and Loathing on the Campaign Trail '72*:

> *There were only two of us in the back: just me and Richard Nixon, and we were talking football in a serious way. . . . It*

*was a very weird trip; probably one of the weirdest things I've ever done, and especially weird because both Nixon and I enjoyed it.*

What's weirder yet is that Nixon might have had greater success than Kennedy as president. He certainly would have handled the Bay of Pigs and the Cuban missile crisis in a more "Luke, I am your father" way. But even the right-wing nut R.T.P. couldn't resist a joyride with Handsome Jack. Just don't let him take you through Dallas by way of Dealey Plaza.

*Bullroaring longhorn LBJ vs. Barry "nuke 'em" Goldwater*

Here the R.T.P. was just plain wrong. Beneath the good ol' boy facade of Lyndon Johnson was Lyndon Johnson. And Goldwater, in retrospect, looks like a man with incorruptible political principles that leave modern Republican candidates asking, "How much do *those* cost?"

*Richard Nixon vs. Hubert Humphrey*

The problem was all of Lyndon Johnson's luggage that Hubert Humphrey was carrying. There wouldn't have been any room for beer in the car.

*Tricky Dick vs. George McGovern*

McGovern's first pick for VP, Thomas Eagleton, was a veteran of road trips with George and had to have electroshock therapy.

*Jimmy Carter* vs. *Jerry Ford*

The R.T.P. was wrong again. Really wrong. So wrong that I don't know how to explain it. Jerry Ford was a star football player at the University of Michigan, on a team that was undefeated for two straight seasons. The Wolverines know how to party! And his wife had a great stash of pills. Jimmy Carter was a born-again peanut farmer. We wouldn't even get any cashews in the cocktail mix. Or any cocktails either. Maybe we weren't paying attention and got him mixed up with his brother Billy.

*Happy-go-lucky Ron* vs. *persimmon-puss Jimmy*

Hollywood, here we come!

*Reagan* vs. *Whoever that stiff was*

Hollywood, here we come again!

*George H. W. Bush* vs. *"I have to go take a Dukakis"*

The phrase in quotations is a word-for-word off-the-record quote from Bush 41 obtained on deep background.

*Bill Clinton* vs. *George Bush*

"Toga! Toga!" to quote Bill's Washington colleague Senator John Blutarsky.

*The guy in the Viagra ads* vs. *The guy getting his food laced with saltpeter by Hillary*

Maybe Bill Clinton wasn't the sane choice over Bob Dole, but he was the *insane* choice. Party on, dude.

*The frat boy from Yale's DKE Animal House* vs. *Al Gore, nickname "Albert"*

No need to read the SparkNotes on this one.

*W.* vs. *John Kerry*

Kerry would have been ordering Châteauneuf-du-Pape ('90) at the Billy Goat Tavern in Chicago; wondering where the Ritz-Carlton was located in Tucumcari, New Mexico; and worrying about getting stone chips on his BMW 7 Series.

*Barack Obama* vs. *John McCain*

The R.T.P was really, really wrong yet another time. One was a fighter pilot. The other flew an adjunct professor of constitutional law's speaker lectern.

*Obama* vs. *Mitt Romney, a Mormon*

Wearing special underpants that, according to LDS church literature, provide "protection against temptation and evil."

*Smilin' Joe Biden* vs. *All the other Republican and Democratic candidates running for president*

But far be it from me to tell the Democrats how to win. It's the Democratic Party's political funeral. I'll gladly decorate the grave. As soon as I get the six-pack out of the cooler in the trunk.

# 10
# The Walking Dead

*Halloween 2015*

Hey, kids! Looking for a swell Halloween zombie costume? Look no farther than your nearest political poll.

You'll see all sorts of rotting corpses lurching around frightfully when they should be six feet under. Bobby Jindal, Rick Santorum, John Kasich, Martin O'Malley, Lindsey Graham, Jim Webb, and George Pataki are all polling below the plus-or-minus margin of undead error.

They're soulless (they're politicians). And they want to eat your brains (because they don't have any of their own or they would have dropped out months ago).

Deceased candidate costumes are easy to make. Get one of Dad's dress shirts, rumple it artfully to give yourself the "common touch," and roll up its sleeves and wear a loosened necktie to look like a "regular guy." Then smear yourself with political gore. (The "Al Gore" kind will do.) No need for masks, since these Creatures from the Campaign Crypt do not have any distinguishing features.

Bonus! As a 2016 zombie presidential candidate, you can trick-or-treat at the houses in your neighborhood *and* at town hall meetings, VFW posts, volunteer firemen's spaghetti dinners, and evangelical churches.

The downside is that you might get spaghetti, a Bible, or two delegates to the Republican National Convention instead of candy.

Why weren't these candidates buried at the ballot crossroads with electoral stakes through their hearts?

Bobby Jindal, the one who looks like a nervous 7-Eleven night shift manager, was in the race to prove that Republicans just *love* diversity. As long as the diverse person is prosperous, doesn't talk funny, and dresses like a Republican the way Ben Carson does. Memo to Bobby and Ben from Reince Priebus, chairman of the Republican National Committee: It's all right if you have some cousins who own fleabag motels or sell crack, but it isn't necessary to bring them with you to the country club.

Republicans talk a good social conservative game, and Rick Santorum is the Republican voice of social conservatism. He's against abortion, illegal immigrants, and gay marriage and in favor of church. And so are all of us Republicans—until our kid knocks up the fifteen-year-old next door, the house needs painting, offending the LBGT community means coming home from the hairdresser with a skunk stripe dyed into our hair, and Christ conflicts with tee time.

John Kasich is the conservative governor of Ohio, a state as purple as Barney the dinosaur.

*Barney's friends are big and small.*
*They come from lots of places.*

And they all hate each other. The conflicts in the Buck-
eye State mirror America's: intransigent labor subjecting
greedy management to extortion, indignant blacks clashing with angry white trash about who can behave more
antisocially, illegal immigrants taking jobs away from illiterate nativists who won't get a job, Tea Party crackpots
vying with liberal dingbats for space on Internet wacko
sites, and the dirty poor dumping on the filthy rich sling-
ing muck at the grubbing-to-get-by middle class. But they
all get along with Kasich.

Kasich beat incumbent moderate Democrat governor Ted Strickland and was reelected by a landslide.
Before Kasich was governor he served nine terms in
Congress shoveling important shinola—eighteen years
on the House Armed Services Committee and six years
as chairman of the House Budget Committee. And Kasich was well liked by colleagues on both sides of the
aisle.

So no wonder he was polling at 2 percent among likely
Republican voters and ended up unable to win a primary
anywhere but in his own backyard. The GOP was in no
damn mood for competent, experienced politicians with
broad popular appeal.

John Kasich is a two-word Republican suicide note.

Martin O'Malley is the ex-governor of Maryland, a
state with no excuse for itself. If you lop off Maryland's
Washington suburbs you're left with Appalachia in the
west, the impoverished fishing villages of the Delmarva
Peninsula (Corsica without the sunshine) in the east, and
Baltimore, Afghanistan on the Patapsco.

Baltimore is grossly impoverished, it has a homicide
rate 26 percent higher than Detroit's, and ABC News

called it the "heroin capital of the United States." O'Malley was its mayor.

After rising to the dignity of governor, O'Malley hiked Maryland taxes by 14 percent, passed traffic speed camera legislation, and repealed the death penalty. (The people who committed Baltimore's 270 murders so far this year say, "Thank you, Marty.")

Maybe O'Malley was playing the same game of "Truth or Dare" that Rick Perry was playing and had to run for president rather than answer the question "How bad do the Ravens suck?"

Senator Lindsey Graham of South Carolina is too hawkish to appeal to the general electorate and not crazy enough to appeal to Republicans. Maybe he thought he could gain support from "progressives," a group that is— to judge by Bernie Sanders's rallies—currently larger and more stupid than usual.

Lindsey's strategy was to have a girl's name, tricking progressives into thinking they were voting for America's first transgender president.

Jim Webb had dropped out of the Democratic presidential race, but he was still trying to scare us by threatening to run as an independent.

As a Democrat, Webb was a strange candidate—a marine, a highly decorated Vietnam vet, President Reagan's secretary of the navy, and a former senator from Virginia. In other words, as a Democrat, he was a Republican.

Maybe Webb is suffering from memory loss. This is a plus. More than 5.3 million Americans suffer from memory loss. That's about the same as Obama's popular vote margin of victory over the Romney zombie in 2012. As a third-party candidate, Webb could have been a factor in the 2016 election. If he'd remembered to run.

Or maybe you kids don't want to be political zombies on Halloween. Maybe too many catatonic creepy creatures are already stalking the streets (and the hustings, campaign stumps, and obscure political blogs). In that case you could dress up as the Invisible Man.

Once, long, long ago, there was a Republican governor of New York state. His name was George Elmer "Fudd" Pataki.

There's a scary story about Elmer Fudd Pataki. One day he mysteriously disappeared from politics. And he never returned. Now some people say he ran for president. *But no one ever saw him!*

# 11
# Time to Pull the Plug on Ben Carson's Campaign

*November 2015*

There is nary a word to be said against Dr. Ben Carson, except by us persnickety fact-checking political pundit types.

Dr. Carson is a soft-spoken gentleman of civilized refinement. He is broadly educated, highly skilled, widely accomplished, and universally respected. And he rose from a background of social adversity and economic deprivation that makes President Obama look like the lost Bush brother.

Thus Ben Carson made us feel small, "us" being the part of America filled with funk and failure and known as political pundits.

We pundits did our best to cut Ben Carson down to size. But we might as well have been George Washington with the cherry tree if George had the body mass index of an Olsen twin, George's little hatchet were a butter knife, and the tree were a mighty oak.

Here, quoted from an *AP* political analysis piece, are two typical failures at attempting to throw Ben Carson into the snark tank.

> "... *a gaff-prone novice lacking a national profile and any significant political network.*"

In other words Ben Carson is a person who says what he thinks, he hasn't spent decades screwing the pooch in Washington or flying his ass from the media flagpole, and he isn't friends with the pack rats running through the sewers of democracy.

> "... *rough around the edges and has little experience with issues beyond health care and business, particularly foreign policy* ..."

That is to say, when Carson gets a baby thrust at him he's more likely to check its vital signs than kiss it. He knows enough to talk about things when he knows what he's talking about. And he doesn't have a clue what the overseas bouquet of assholes is going to do next because nobody does.

Indeed, to hear any worthwhile skepticism about Ben Carson's presidential campaign, we had to go to the good doctor himself. He said, "The likelihood of someone like me getting through this process and making it to president is virtually impossible."

Republican primary voters—a group with well-attested mental health issues—were responding to treatment by Dr. Ben. In polls during the late fall of 2015, support for Carson rose from 6 percent to 23 percent, putting him (given political polling's 100 percent +/– margin of error) in a dead heat with Donald Trump for GOP front-runner.

In Freudian terms, there was an upside to Republican schizophrenia. The Republican id favored *id*iotic Donald Trump. But the Republican superego went for superior Ben Carson.

(Dr. Carson, being a neurosurgeon, probably favors a physiological and biochemical model of brain dysfunction over a Freudian model. This means he was a shoo-in for the presidential nomination if Republicans stayed on their meds. Which they didn't.)

Ben Carson in brief:

Raised in inner-city Detroit by an illiterate single mother who worked as a domestic, sometimes with three jobs at once, so that Ben and his brother Curtis could (no, *would*—she didn't give them a choice) go to college. (Curtis is now a senior executive with Honeywell.)

Ben Carson has said, only somewhat jokingly, that his mother ought to be the woman with her face on the new $10 bill. (If it's Eleanor Roosevelt's, every currency scanner in the country will break.)

Ben went to Yale and the University of Michigan Medical School and completed his residency in neurosurgery at Johns Hopkins, where he became the hospital's youngest-ever director of pediatric neurosurgery at age thirty-three in 1984—when Donald Trump was laying the foundation for his first bankruptcy at Atlantic City's Trump Plaza casino, Jeb Bush was chairing meetings of the Dade County Republican

Party in a phone booth, Carly Fiorina was in the break room making coffee for AT&T executives, and Marco Rubio was in eighth grade.

Dr. Carson was the first surgeon to successfully separate Siamese twins conjoined at the head. He has thirty-eight honorary doctorate degrees in addition to his real one. And he has received the nation's highest civilian honor, the Presidential Medal of Freedom.

This was why, in November 2015, I was asking Dr. Ben Carson *to please quit running for president.*

Get back to work, damn it! We need you. George W.'s and Jeb's heads might get conjoined. True, they're not twins. But the Bush family is inbred, and freakish things can result from inbreeding.

Yes, you've retired from surgery. You feel, I gather, that the hand-eye coordination and three-dimensional reasoning to which you credit your excellence as a surgeon will decline in your sixties. Hand-eye coordination is unnecessary for a chief executive. That's what Vice President Fiorina operating the Keurig single-cup in the Oval Office pantry is for. And what use is three-dimensional reasoning in a job dealing with one-dimensional people?

But, Dr. Ben, you could be teaching others what you know. You're not only a doctor; you're a professor. You've taught pediatrics, oncology, neurosurgery, and plastic surgery. Right now you could be teaching some young plastic surgeon how to remove Donald Trump's ruptured gel-filled silicone brain implant that is endangering Republicans everywhere.

Dr. Carson, you are valuable. Presidential candidates are not.

Politics is the career that we Americans who, like your mother, are trying to be good parents choose for our *loser* children.

Many of us have sons and daughters who will not get into medical school or start a business, join the military, learn a trade, raise a family, perform needful volunteer work, or do anything else that has even the slightest value to society such as follow a Phish tribute band around the country selling artisanal hacky sacks outside concert venues. These children we send into politics.

Second, Dr. Carson, there is the matter of whether you're good at politics. You are a good man. This would argue to the contrary.

You're a good man with good values who's good at doing good things and you have, in my opinion, good ideas. It is impossible for me to envision a place for you in Washington.

At the moment it may seem as if you're good at politics. You're getting a good measure of support for being a "Washington outsider."

But politics is not the art of being—let alone doing—good.

And every art, no matter how dark, requires skill and practice.

How good would you feel about a surgical procedure conducted by an "operating room outsider"—someone who didn't know a hemostat from a thermostat, a curette from a lamb cutlet, forceps from "Fore!" or a retractor from John Deere?

If you won the Republican nomination, you'd be running against Hillary Clinton or Joe Biden or maybe Martin O'Malley or Jim Webb (not Bernie Sanders—he's still wanted on a House Un-American Activities Committee subpoena from 1961).

These quacks have been in the Washington political operating theater for a long time. They're splattered with gore from the butchery they've committed on their hapless patient, the body politic. Severed limbs of liberty litter the floor. Ventricles, atria, and the aorta have been ripped out and tossed beneath the heart-lung machine of federal bureaucracy. Intestinal fortitude has been disemboweled and the viscera of nationhood spill forth and hang, dripping offal, from the arms of the nurses of liberalism while the sawbones drink the tax dollar lifeblood of America from the IV fluid drip. The mask of anesthesia has been clamped upon the electorate's face. Vital signs have flatlined.

Dr. Carson, you're not going in there and successfully separating any conjoined anything. In fact, one peek and you're going to be back out in the hallway of the palliative care hospice that America has become, puking your guts out.

If it's any comfort, this would make us political pundits feel better.

# 12
# In Memoriam

To Our Presidential Campaign Fallen:
*Let Whatshisface, Whoizis, and Wuddayacallit
Never Be Forgotten*

$A$nother year has passed, and so have the dreams and wishes of many 2016 POTUS hopefuls. It is only fitting that we pay them our final respects.

(And, also, my condolences to the reader for, after just two chapters, my making fun of dead candidates again. In the study of folklore this is called a "joke cycle." Often the cycles reoccur rapidly. This has happened with the "dead baby" joke cycle that began in the early 1960s. Personally, I find the "dead candidate" joke cycle funnier. *What's the difference between a truck full of dead candidates and a truck full of bowling balls? You can't unload a truck full of bowling balls with a pitchfork.*)

## Scott Walker

### *July 13, 2015–September 21, 2015*

Fare thee well, you dreamy, idealistic youth. So long to America's chance to have a president who gets carded every time he orders a beer, even in the White House Mess.

Walker was a great campaigner. He was so good at running for governor of Wisconsin that he even ran against himself in the 2012 Wisconsin gubernatorial recall election. And won!

Governor Walker fought Wisconsin's powerful unions—the Cow Union; the Cheese Union; the United Federation of Walleye, Smallmouth Bass, Perch, and Northern Pike; and the Amalgamated Brotherhood of People Wearing Funny Hats at Green Bay Packer Games.

Walker was once considered a front-runner for the GOP nomination. Then, in an attempt to, as it were, "Trump" the other Republican candidates, Walker proposed that we build a wall not only along the Mexican border but also along the border with Canada.

I predict Scott Walker will have the last laugh as America is flooded with smuggled maple syrup, pulpwood, Hudson Bay blankets, and immigrants competing for American jobs the way Ted Cruz, born in Calgary, has competed for the American job of being president of America.

## Lindsey Graham

### *June 1, 2015–December 12, 2015*

Support for Lindsey Graham's presidential candidacy was limited—to Lindsey Graham. Even his wife wouldn't vote for him and that's only partly because he isn't married.

Conservatives didn't like Graham because he's soft on climate change, gun control, and immigration.

Liberals didn't like Graham because he's strong for NSA, Gitmo, and American military intervention overseas.

Then Graham alienated everybody else by going on *Face the Nation* and saying, "Congress might have to explore the need to limit some forms of freedom of speech."

Members of Congress didn't need to bother. The American people did it for them, responding to Graham's speeches with, "Oh, shut up."

Graham positioned himself as a "Reagan-style Republican," forgetting one key aspect of Ronald Reagan: He's dead. And so is Lindsey Graham's presidential campaign.

## Lawrence Lessig

*September 6, 2015–November 2, 2015*

What was the problem with Democratic presidential candidate Lawrence Lessig?

Was it being a professor at Harvard Law School? Voters forgave Barack Obama for being at Harvard Law School.

Was it opposing laws protecting intellectual property rights? That would make all of Harvard's intellectual property free. A fair price.

Was it wanting to convene a Second Constitutional Convention when, after 229 years, we're still not done arguing about the first one?

You say, "No, the problem with Boris Blessing . . . Doris Lessing . . . Lawrence of Arabia . . . the St. Lawrence

Seaway . . . Larry the Cable Guy . . . Who *are* we talking about?" And you've put your finger on it.

## Jim Webb

*July 2, 2015–October 20, 2015*

Speaking of utterly forgotten Democratic presidential contenders, did somebody say something about Jim Webb?

Nope.

## Bobby Jindal

*June 24, 2015–November 17, 2015*

Bobby Jindal's run for president proved that the GOP isn't just a club for dumb white guys. Or, anyway, it proved that *anybody* can be a dumb white guy these days, e.g., Chaz Bono.

Bobby Jindal is the best governor Louisiana has ever had—the blue-ribbon show pig at the Mecca Livestock Roundup.

For instance, when Hurricane Katrina did not strike New Orleans while Jindal was governor, New Orleans was not destroyed.

Jindal improved his state's bond rating, cut the state deficit, and did not get sent to jail as is customary for Louisiana politicians.

Jindal dropped out of the presidential race to avoid bringing shame on his family. Jindal's father is a civil engineer and his mother is a nuclear physicist. And here was their son Bobby, who'd showed so much promise, looking for a job shoveling America's trash in the Oval Office.

## Rick Perry

*June 4, 2015–September 11, 2015*

Rick Perry has forgotten more than the other candidates will ever know about cutting the size and cost of the federal government. Literally forgotten, as in the November 2011 GOP presidential candidate debate, where he promised to eliminate three government agencies and then couldn't remember which.

But Perry had been running so hard in the 2012 presidential race that even after he ran into a wall of mud (full name, Mitt Romney) he kept on going—right off the edge of the cliff in the 2016 presidential race. Then he hung in midair for a while, legs flailing.

Perry wears glasses to look intellectual. He should have used the glasses to watch what happens to Wile E. Coyote in *Road Runner* cartoons.

## Lincoln Chafee

*June 3, 2015–October 23, 2015*

Lincoln is so unmemorable that his rich WASP mother—with stylish debutante absentmindedness—forgot to name him. A couple of years after he was born Mummy was pulling a five out of her purse to pay the gardener and the gardener asked, "What's the kid called?"

Chafee's middle name is Davenport. As in . . .

*Chafee père: "Who's that on the davenport?"*

*Chafee mère: "Davenport?"*

Lincoln does not have much of a memory himself. He can't remember what party he belongs to. He said he was a Republican when he ran for the Senate in 2000, but then he voted the Democratic Party line so well that the American Conservative Union gave him a rating of 12 out of 100. Senator Barack Obama got an ACU rating of 17.

After Chafee lost his Senate seat to a real Democrat in 2006, LinkedIn became an "independent." An independent is a person who doesn't know what to think. And is proud of it.

Chafee was governor of America's most insignificant state. The list of famous people born in Rhode Island begins with one Farrelly brother and ends with the other. The poverty rate is 0.7 percent higher than that in West Virginia. The economy is the same size as Uzbekistan's. Rhode Island ranks forty-eighth in state GDP, avoiding fiftieth place only because all the Vermonters are stoned with their faces buried in tubs of Ben & Jerry's Cherry Garcia, and nobody lives in Montana.

Rhode Island fields no major-league sports teams. Its most prominent university hasn't played in a bowl game since 1916. (Rose Bowl final: Brown 0, Washington State 14.) Culturally, Rhode Island once had a bad nightclub fire. Local cuisine features clam cake, quahog chowder, snail salad, and pizza without cheese.

A Chafee—something between a wedgie and a noogie.

## George Pataki

*May 28, 2015–December 29, 2015*

George Pataki is a political hack. The only novelty being that the hackney cab of his career has been pulled by an elephant instead of a donkey.

Pataki served four terms in the New York state assembly. ("Don't tell Mother I'm a New York state assemblyman; she thinks I play piano in a house of ill repute.")

As New York's governor Pataki cut a few taxes and curtailed some spending. Moody's credit rating for the state went up (just in time for the 2008 fiscal crisis, to show what Moody's knows).

Pataki approved Native American casinos in places like Buffalo. "The food sucks, no real restaurant or entertainment," reads a Yelp review of Buffalo Creek Casino.

With the fair and balanced approach that being a hack requires, Pataki lobbied for gay rights and opposed gay marriage.

Pataki promised he'd serve only two terms. He served three.

Pataki privatized the World Trade Center—a few weeks before the 9/11 attacks. (Truther alert.)

And Pataki signed some of the nation's toughest gun control laws, causing fellow Republicans to tell him where to conceal his weapon.

Pataki is one of a long line of New York Republican moderates—moderately honest, moderately stupid. He joins the ranks of "those who've gone before" such as the previously mentioned Nelson Rockefeller, a minor vice of a vice president, and Thomas "Dewey defeats Truman" Dewey.

Pataki never came close to getting that much media attention. His only moment in the national limelight was during his inauguration as governor. Howard Stern stood next to him on the podium.

So we bid adieu to these well-qualified men—or sort of well-qualified or maybe qualified, or not—who boldly sacrificed, um, spending more time with their families, to serve their nation. That is, to hang around waiting to be asked to serve their nation meanwhile blotting the landscape with ugly yard signs, pestering voters with dinnertime robocalls, and raising money from dopes.

Here's your hat, what's your hurry? Don't let the door hit you in the ass on your way out.

# 13
# Our Higgledy-Piggledy Primary System and How It Higgles Our Pigs

*Late January 2016*

The presidential campaign's so-called "primary season" was about to begin. The BBC called me and asked if I could do a brief radio piece explaining America's political primary system. I failed miserably. I couldn't explain the primaries to the British. I couldn't even explain them to myself. There's a good reason for this.

The Democratic Party and the Republican Party may think they are integral parts of the U.S. government, but in fact they're private organizations with no more constitutional standing than motorcycle gangs.

Maybe in 2020 we'll select our two major presidential candidates with fists, chains, and knives in the parking lots of biker bars. In which case expect either Leadhead Eddie of the Bandidos or Gypsy Joker member Bob the Beef to oust the Oval Office incumbent.

For the time being, however, we've got a dumber way of picking who'll run for president. This involves "primaries" and "caucuses." Both Democrats and Republicans have either one or the other in all fifty states and the District of Columbia. (Although until 1961 people who lived in D.C. were considered to be overexposed to the debilitating effects of political radiation and therefore not competent to vote.)

Democrats and Republicans also have primaries and caucuses in American Samoa, Puerto Rico, Guam, the Virgin Islands, and the Northern Marianas to make sure that residents of U.S. territories who don't get to vote in presidential elections have a say in who they don't get to vote for.

The primaries have different rules depending on your location. It's a baseball game where if you're on first base you're supposed to dunk the ball through the net, if you're on second base you're supposed to knock the puck past the goalie, and if you're on third base you're supposed to kick a field goal.

Caucuses are coffee klatches for people who need to find a bingo game.

State and territorial primaries and caucuses take place at different times. Each is scheduled to be either so early that who you vote for doesn't matter or so late that it doesn't matter how you vote.

Who's in charge of this process? Nobody. Because that's who's in charge of the Democratic and Republican parties. The Democratic and Republican national organizations aren't in charge because they're run by the Democratic and Republican party state organizations, who aren't in charge because they're run by the Democratic and Republican party county organizations. There are 3,143 counties in the

United States. The Republican party county chairman is a retired Burger King franchisee in double knit slacks with a white vinyl belt and matching shoes, and the Democratic Party county chairman is a woman who owns nineteen cats.

The reason American political parties have no constitutional standing is that the framers of the Constitution hoped America would have no political parties.

In *Federalist Paper* No. 9 Alexander Hamilton declares "domestic faction" to be "the cause of incurable disorder and imbecility in the government."

In *Federalist Paper* No. 10 James Madison inveighs against "the violence of faction," calls it a "dangerous vice," and warns that "the public good is disregarded in the conflict of rival parties."

Madison, admonishing readers about the temptations of party politics, describes, with eerie prescience, our Democratic and Republican presidential primaries and caucuses 228 years in the future:

> So strong is the propensity of mankind to fall into mutual animosities that where no substantial occasion presents itself the most frivolous and fanciful distinctions have been sufficient to kindle their unfriendly passions and excite their most violent conflicts.

However, even in 1788, most Americans weren't listening to Hamilton and Madison. And neither were Hamilton and Madison. Alexander Hamilton would go on to form the Federalist Party. And James Madison would cofound the Democratic-Republican Party with Thomas

Jefferson, who had also claimed to oppose political parties. In a 1789 letter to his friend and fellow signer of the Declaration of Independence, Francis Hopkinson, Jefferson wrote, "If I could not go to heaven but with a party, I would not go there at all."

George Washington detested political parties and didn't belong to one, but by the end of his second term a recognizably modern "two-party system" had taken hold.

This caused George—by solemn Father-of-His-Country standards—to burst a seam. In his 1796 Farewell Address the first president said:

> Let me now . . . warn you in the most solemn manner against the baneful effects of the spirit of party generally. . . . The alternate domination of one faction over another, sharpened by the spirit of revenge, natural to party dissension, which in different ages and countries has perpetrated the most horrid enormities, is itself a frightful despotism. But this leads at length to a more formal and permanent despotism. The disorders and miseries which result gradually incline the minds of men to seek security and repose in the absolute power of an individual.

In other words, Donald Trump. Or, for that matter, Hillary Clinton, supposing she won and carried the Senate and the House.

So, if we were guided by the thoughts of wise men— or of men while they were being temporarily wise— America shouldn't have any political parties. And we'd be spared discussion of primaries, caucuses, and other ridiculous methods by which Democrats and Republicans choose their electoral candidates such as rummaging through the partisan trash to pick superdelegates and delegates-at-large.

America shouldn't have any political parties, and, funnily enough, America doesn't. At least, we don't have any of what most people in most of the world would understand as "political parties."

Thirty-five years ago I was in the Soviet Union, where I became friendly with a reporter from *Pravda*. Friendly enough that I admitted my admiration for Ronald Reagan. One night the reporter and I were in a bar talking about Reagan and Brezhnev. The reporter said, "You are Republican?" I said yes. The reporter leaned in close, lowered his voice, and asked, "Are you *Party Member*?"

In America you don't join a political party, it tries to join you. No major American political party has ever had anything that could be construed as an ideology. The parties usually don't even have more than one or two ideas. You don't pay "dues" unless you want to. I suppose you could be a card-carrying Republican or Democrat, if you got the card printed yourself. There's no such thing as "party discipline," as Bernie Sanders showed. And, as Donald Trump proved, you can't get kicked out of an American political party no matter what you say or do.

In America, instead of political parties, we have two vague political tendencies. One tendency is to favor a larger, more powerful government to make things better. The other tendency is to favor a smaller, more limited government to make things less worse. Then there are a few other vague tendencies—slightly isolationist versus somewhat internationalist, and reasonably pro-business as opposed to moderately in favor of whatever's out-of-business at the moment. Plus a tendency to be hypocritically prudish and exclusive in contrast to a tendency to be cynically inclusive and insist on enforced freethinking.

This makes for a mess of a Venn diagram depicting the logical sets (or, as they should be called in American politics, "illogical sets"). Over time, the Venn diagram sometimes shows extensive overlap of common elements. And sometimes not—2016 being a "not" year. Also, lately, the Venn diagram has been paintballed and TP'd and had rotten fruit thrown at it.

Nonetheless, it can be hard to tell American political parties apart. As my late friend, journalist (and Marxist) Alexander Cockburn, put it, "Americans have a one-party system, and, just like Americans, they have two of them."

The fact that, usually, there's a major American political party claiming to be conservative while, usually, its opposite number is claiming to be otherwise, does not make distinction easier.

For example, the supposedly conservative Federalists were for a great big federal government and an international alliance with Britain. The supposedly liberal Democratic-Republicans had a platform that sounded like George Wallace's—states' rights and "fortress America."


Our political parties were despised to begin with and were given, by law, the role in government they deserve, which is none. The parties themselves are salmagundis, olla podridas, and hash. No wonder the process by which they select their presidential candidates is a repulsive muddle.

Things didn't use to be better. Until the 1830s a presidential candidate was customarily selected by a political party's congressional delegation. We can imagine the insider deals hatched in the era's snuff-filled rooms. The Senate was not at that time directly elected, and the general franchise was severely limited. Voters had about as much say in choosing the presidential nominee as you have in choosing your airline seat when using frequent-flier miles to travel on a holiday weekend.

Nominating conventions were thought to be a more democratic alternative. The first presidential nominating convention was held in 1831 by the Anti-Masonic Party. They were adamantly opposed to Shriners in miniature cars driving around in circus parades. Or something. And that pretty much set the tone for wisdom and intelligence at national political party conventions for the next seventy years.

State and local party bosses quickly took control of the conventions. To wield political influence you no longer had to be anything as elevated as a crooked elected official; merely being crooked would suffice.

Of course there's nothing that can't be worsened by reform. Reformers of the Progressive era took aim at the conventions, seeking to replace them with some type of referendum—a preliminary vote (a "primary") or a public committee meeting (a "caucus")—by which ordinary citizens would select convention delegates.

In 1901 the first state law to create a presidential primary was enacted in, of all places, Florida, which was, then as now . . . you know what I mean . . . Florida. The practice of holding primaries or caucuses spread everywhere like a flutter of hanging chads shaken loose from a tampered-with ballot.

Primaries, in particular, thrived. Twenty states had political primaries by 1920, and by 1992 there were Republican primaries in thirty-nine states and Democratic primaries in forty. Consistency is not a hallmark of American politics, but exceptions are made when the constant is stupidity. Today's primaries are as stupid as they've always been.

The primary-and-caucus system of selecting presidential candidates has prevailed, with results for all to see.

In 2016 congressional delegations were as pointless in the nomination process as they are in Congress. The conventions were simply bad TV commercials, the kind that don't send you to the phone to buy the product; they send you to the phone to call the Better Business Bureau. And the electorate as a whole might as well have been monkeys throwing darts at front pages of the *National Enquirer* and FBI "Wanted" posters.

Only a little more than a quarter of eligible voters cast ballots in Democratic or Republican primaries and caucuses. More than half of the Republicans and nearly half of the Democrats supported candidates other than the two we got. According to figures from the *New York Times* (and, per Donald Trump's accusations against the *New York Times* as part of the liberal vote-rigging scheme, the *New York Times* should know), it was just 14 percent of people who are entitled to vote who gave us Clinton and Trump.

# 14
# A Halfhearted Case for Marco Rubio

*February 5, 2016*

This is how I was feeling four days before the 2016 New Hampshire presidential primary:

I must, I can, I *will* be positive about Marco Rubio. I'm a Republican. Rubio is the least insane candidate (low bar) with the best chance (faint hope) of actually beating Hillary.

The patients have taken over the GOP psychiatric ward. The shrink is on the couch. The loonies are thoughtfully stroking their chins, asking the sane Republican, "*Why* don't you think Barack Hussein Obama, who bows to Mecca five times each day, wasn't cloned by KGB agents in the jungles of Kenya?"

Rubio's all I've got left. Jeb Bush was the Super Bowl Goodyear Blimp of Republican candidates. Then he took his campaign playbook from the John Frankenheimer movie *Black Sunday*. Rand Paul seems to be running for president of Galt's Gulch in Ayn Rand's *Atlas Shrugged*.

Christie, Christie, two-by-four. Can't get through the outhouse door.

John Kasich is polling somewhere to the right of the decimal point in those incommensurable ratios that my Algebra II teacher was talking about before I flunked. The Nabisco graham cracker box has more Twitter followers than the Lindsey Graham cracker does.

(By the way, hats off to the Democrats in this election cycle. They may be stupid but they're not psychotic. They watched Bernie Sanders trying to levitate the Pentagon, gathering signatures on the SDS Port Huron Statement, and making one last, forty-eight-year-late attempt to organize the demonstrators in Grant Park outside the site of the 1968 Democratic National Convention, and they said, "Nope, nominate the lying old fishwife.")

OK, what's really great about Marco Rubio is . . .

Don't rush me. . . .

### Marco Rubio is a Washington outsider!

Well, actually, he's a U.S. senator. But he's missed a lot of Senate votes, and I assume that was because, during the voting, Rubio was *outside* Washington. This counts.

### Marco Rubio's finances are a mess!

Rubio owns houses that he has trouble paying for. We, the American people, own two houses (of Congress) and a White House that we have trouble paying for.

Rubio emptied his retirement account to meet current expenses. This is exactly the way Social Security works.

Rubio bought a boat he couldn't afford. The U.S. Navy does that all the time.

When it comes to the federal budget, Rubio is the man with the plan.

**Marco Rubio has an impressive legislative record!**

Despite being a Washington outsider and missing a lot of Senate votes, Marco Rubio has shown bold leadership introducing vital legislation in Congress:

S.124    A bill to amend the Water Resources Development Act of 1996 to deauthorize the Ten Mile Creek Water Preserve Area Critical Restoration Project in the South Florida Water Management District

S.1403    Florida Fisheries Improvement Act

S.RES.112    A resolution expressing the sense of the Senate that the Internal Revenue Service should provide printed copies of Internal Revenue Service Publication 17 to taxpayers in the United States free of charge

This is to name but a few of the Senate bills, amendments, and resolutions bearing Marco Rubio's name.

**Marco Rubio earned his success the old-fashioned American way!**

By sucking up to rich people, specifically Governor Jeb Bush of Florida. Bush advised Rubio on how to present himself to conservative voters, nurtured Rubio's rise from Miami city commissioner to speaker of the house in the Florida state legislature, cultivated wealthy donors on Rubio's behalf, and backed Rubio's 2010 U.S. Senate run. Then Rubio turned around and kicked Jeb in the balls. And what's more American than that?

**Marco Rubio gets the Latino vote!**

In Cuba. If Cuba had political polls, Marco Rubio would be polling far ahead of Raúl Castro in the Cuban presidential election, if Cuba had elections.

**Marco Rubio gets the youth vote!**

As long as we can convince mush-head millennials that Rubio's suit, tie, and local-news-anchor-haircut look is "ironic."

We'll also tell the millennials that Rubio has a full sleeve of tats under his French cuffs. And that Rubio was doing antiabortion rants just to punk Ted Cruz in Iowa. Plus let's remind millennials that Hillary Clinton is such a fossil she could be Rubio's mother.

Which gives me an idea for getting Rubio some media play. Rubio was born in May 1971. Do the math. In September 1970, *where was Bill Clinton*?

Maybe in Miami on Yale Law School's extra-early spring break?

**Marco Rubio is Bill Clinton's love child!**

That should go viral.

**Marco Rubio is a fun swimming pool game for the whole GOP candidate slate!**

The candidate who's "it" keeps his eyes firmly shut (the way GOP voters are doing). When he or she yells "Marco" all the other candidates have to yell "Rubio." Then the candidate who's "it"—using nothing but the sound of the other players' voices—tries to catch another candidate and tag him or her. Whoever gets tagged is out of the pool. Right away we'll get rid of Donald Trump, with all that hair dragging in the water behind him.

**And that has inspired me to write a Marco Rubio television campaign ad that will make my fortune as a political consultant!**

Marco Rubio stands beside a beautiful Olympic-sized South Beach swimming pool with an American flag painted on the bottom. The pool is filled with a young, attractive, vivacious, multicultural crowd of Tea Party supporters, Right-to-Lifers, tax cut advocates, Evangelical Christians (they can wear modest one-piece bathing suits), Second Amendment enthusiasts, and members of the 1%. The candidate closes his eyes and shouts, "Marco!" Everyone responds with loud enthusiasm, "Rubio!" Marco cannonballs into the deep end. The campaign slogan appears on the screen:

**When Washington Is All Wet**
**Rubio Will Make a Big Splash!!!**

# 15
# The Case Against
# Marco Rubio

*February 6, 2016*

And this is what I was hearing three days before the 2016 New Hampshire presidential primary:

Remarks by Senator Marco Rubio taken from the transcript of the February 6 Republican presidential candidates' debate at Saint Anselm College in Manchester, New Hampshire.

*And let's dispel once and for all with this fiction that Barack Obama doesn't know what he's doing. He knows exactly what he's doing. . . . But I would add this. Let's dispel with this fiction that Barack Obama doesn't know what he's doing. He knows exactly what he's doing. . . . Here's the bottom line. This notion that Barack Obama doesn't know what he's doing is just not true. He knows exactly what he's doing.*

# 16
# Cruz Control

*A March 2016 Plea to America's Youth!*

Now is the time for all good millennials to come to the aid of their country!

Young people of the United States, you must save our nation. America's old people have gone insane. Look who they're supporting for president.

The 2016 presidential campaign is the most severe case of American mass psychosis since the Salem witch trials of 1692. In fact, it's worse. What kind of witch hunt leaves Goodwife Hillary not dunked in a pond, not pressed under stones, not fastened by the ankles in the it-takes-a-village stocks?

And Hillary is, arguably, the front-running candidate possessed by the *fewest* demons. (Although watching her head spin around while she spews campaign vomit is scary.)

Enter Ben Carson. Cauldron boiling.

*Eye of Newt (Gingrich), facts of fog,*

*Hare of brain, tongue of blog*

Bernie Sanders taketh innocent voters up into an exceeding high mountain and showeth them all the kingdoms of the world, and the glory of them; And sayeth unto them, All these things will I give thee, plus free tuition.

And then there's Trump—Landlord of the Flies.

No one knows what caused mature adult Americans to lose their minds. Maybe it's long-overdue LSD flashbacks from the 1960s. Perhaps sharing cat videos on Facebook is an Alzheimer's trigger. Or it could be post-traumatic stress disorder from when you kids came home with flesh plugs in your earlobes.

Anyway, crazy old people are to blame for the presidential front-runners. Who else answers the phone when "A-Hole Political Pollster" appears on caller ID?

And crazy old people will be to blame for whichever spawn of Satan slithers its way into the Oval Office.

The whole electoral process is in the hands of don't-trust-anyone-over-the-age-I-was-under-when-I-was-saying-don't-trust-anyone-over-that-age.

Eighty-six percent of Republicans and voters who "lean Republican" are on the wrong side of thirty. That doesn't make the Blue States hip and happening. Eighty-two percent of Democrats and voters who "lean Democratic" are likewise.

People who actually vote in presidential elections are, on average, nearly fifty. The highest voter turnout is among those who are sixty-plus.

But before we have presidential elections we have presidential primaries.

You young people don't vote much, and when it comes to primaries, you don't vote in droves.

"Primaries?" you ask. "Whoa, what are they, *primarily*?" Then you say, "What's up with them being all whenever and wherever, during weird months in states I've never heard of?" And, "Is there an app for that?"

*Nobody* votes in primaries. In 2012, when the entire country was supposedly full of the political hots and bothers, just 15.9 percent of the electorate cast a primary vote. We don't know how old these primary-voting nobodies are, but I'm guessing their average age is dead.

Brain-dead, for certain.

Therefore I'm asking you young people to make an enormous sacrifice. I'm asking you to find a presidential primary and vote in it.

But that's not all I'm asking. I'm asking you to make a much greater sacrifice, a terrible sacrifice.

I'm asking you to find a *Republican* presidential primary and vote in it.

Here's why.

Americans over thirty are such deranged maniacs that Hillary Clinton might not be heinous and abominable enough for them. A Republican front-runner could be elected.

You say, "Oh, go on, get outta here." Surely Ben Carson will be checking himself into the memory care facility soon. And it can't be long before Donald Trump is exposed as a double agent and goes into hiding at the Chappaqua safe house, or wherever it is Hillary has Bill stashed.

But now there is *another* Republican. Ted Cruz. As of mid-March he's only six points behind Donald Trump and closing.

And Cruz could be electable. He's got the crazy thing going for him, but it's crazy like a fox or, anyway, like Fox

News. In contrast to Carson, Cruz knows who's buried in Lenin's tomb. And, in contrast to Trump, he isn't angling to get a sweetheart deal on a hotel and casino in Raqqah as a reward for inflaming anti-American hatred worldwide.

Ted Cruz could beat Hillary Clinton. He's 161 years younger than she is—in dog years. Dogs are all we've got this election cycle, so it's a fair measure.

Cruz has a national political record going back only as far as his Senate race in 2013. Clinton is dragging a hundred miles of public policy toilet-paper-trail stuck to her campaign shoe.

Hillary reminds every man in America of his first wife. Voters are 47.9 percent male. And 47.9 happens to be exactly the percent of the popular vote that won George W. Bush the presidency in 2000.

We need Cruz Control.

I know, I know, you young people are saying, "P. J., you're an elderly and unhinged Republican yourself. What's up with getting your plaid XL boxers in a wad over Ted Cruz? Isn't he your kind of guy?"

No, he's not. I mean, OK, yes, I like Ted's flat tax idea—the same clever plan for tax reform that put Steve Forbes in the White House in 1996.

And usually I am, like Ted, opposed to stricter gun controls. But according to Wikipedia Cruz told radio host Hugh Hewitt, "The simple fact is the overwhelming majority of violent criminals are Democrats." So maybe gun purchase background checks should include a question about party affiliation.

Cruz seems a little clueless on foreign policy. I don't think carpet bombing ISIS will work. Didn't they pretty much invent the carpet over there?

Cruz doesn't believe in climate change. That's nonsense. I've been around for a long time. Climate change is real. Temperatures go up in the summer and down in the winter every year.

Cruz opposes legalization of marijuana. I have two teenage daughters. I worry about them. And marijuana is a drug that makes teenage boys drive slow.

The rest of Ted Cruz's platform is just the standard-issue delusional right-wing raving that keeps anyone to the left of me (and practically everybody is) from even thinking about voting Republican.

Take a Thorazine or something, Ted, and stop the anti-immigrant rants. I'm sixty-nine. What am I supposed to do, raise my own children? Plus, you're practically a wetback yourself, Ted, or would be if there were a river between Alberta and Texas. You Canadian, you.

And stop the antiabortion rants. As I mentioned, I've got teenage daughters. If abortion laws need any tweaking, it's this: The woman gets to decide what to do with the baby. And I get to decide what to do with the boyfriend.

But where Ted Cruz goes completely off the rails is when he refuses to criticize Donald Trump. *Refuses to criticize Donald Trump?* That's inconceivable. That's impossible. That's like . . . like . . . Lady Gaga refuses to wear an outfit because it's too out there. Like Ben and Jerry refuse to sell Leonardo DiCappuccino Ice Cream. Simile fails me.

I'm *ethnically* Republican. (I know you young people understand identity politics.) My grandmother was born in the nineteenth century near Springfield, Illinois, where the only Democrat anybody had ever heard of was John Wilkes Booth.

If you're an ethnic Republican the way I am, born and bred in the Republican Party, what Donald Trump is . . .

Suppose you're an ethnic Scot, born and bred in Scotland, and you go see *Austin Powers: The Spy Who Shagged Me* and watch Mike Myers playing "Fat Bastard." *That's* how Donald Trump looks to me.

And when Trump Tower burns, Ted Cruz plans to be playing fireman—on the sidewalk with the safety net, catching all the Trump voters when they leap.

Please, please help put a regular doofus Republican on the ballot.

I know you young people are comfortable with Hillary Clinton. She's familiar. You're used to her. She's the spitting image of the worn-out, bitter, sarcastic second-wave feminist adjunct professor teaching your gender studies class. Easy A, if you can wade through the Betty Friedan crap.

But what if America decides to drop that course? What if Americans just can't stand another minute of Clinton smug and Clinton smirk?

Every presidential election needs two candidates, neither of whom will cause you to leap off a bridge or move to Ted Cruz's Canada if the other one wins.

When America doesn't have two candidates like that, bad things happen.

In 1968 one candidate was Hubert Humphrey. He was a doofus and LBJ's doormat and nobody really liked him. But he was mostly harmless.

The Republicans also could have run a doofus nobody really liked. They had plenty available, such as Mitt Romney's dad George. But they failed to nominate someone who was mostly harmless.

Instead, He-Who-Must-Not-Be-Named, Richard Nixon, won the election. And pay attention here: 1968 was the first time eighteen-year-olds had voting rights.

Young people of today, don't let this happen to you.

You have the power. There are 53.5 million of you between the ages of eighteen and twenty-nine. There were only 32.9 million primary voters in 2012 (total, Republicans and Democrats). You have a 163 percent advantage.

Just pick any regular doofus Republican polling below 13 percent—Rubio, Paul, Kasich, Fiorina, Pataki, the Jebster, whatever. They're mostly harmless.

They're definitely harmless compared with the crazy old people currently in control of the whole electoral process.

If you don't do something, crazy old people will be running the world.

Wait . . .

*Why are you young people looking at me that way? It's freaking me out. You're trying to control my mind. I can tell by your strange facial hair. You're broadcasting mind control microwaves from your lip studs. The aliens who abducted me last night were talking about it. They've got Elvis too. Maybe I can protect myself if I line my hat with tinfoil. You're all members of the Trilateral Commission, aren't you? And the Council on Foreign Relations. And the Rosicrucians. I saw your New World Order black helicopters hovering over my carport.*

Fortunately here's a man in a cocked hat with one hand thrust inside his jacket offering to help me. He suggests that I take a job as an off-season caretaker at a snowbound hotel in the Rocky Mountains and use the

time to write an exposé that will put an end to your secret
conspiracy with Ted Cruz.

```
All work and no play makes Trump president
All work and no play makes Trump president
All work and no play makes Trump president
All work and no play makes Trump president
All work and no play makes Trump president
```

# 17
# Fashion Notes

*The Candidates Will All Fry in Perdition.*
*The Question Is, Are They Dressed for the Occasion?*

We tried delving deep into the hearts and minds of the candidates. We endeavored to look into their souls. We attempted to ponder their abilities, their experience, and their policy positions. What an awful experience. Maybe we should be more superficial. Let's look at what the candidates were wearing.

Personally, I'm no arbiter of style. I'm a navy blue/ banker gray, J. Press, barrel cuff, club tie duffer who buys a new suit when I start to see my knees between my trouser pinstripes. But like most males of a certain age who'd rather appear in public with a lampshade on our head than in a collarless shirt, I can tell you what message a person's clothing conveys.

Mark Twain said, "Clothes make the man. Naked people have little or no influence on society."

How wrong Twain was. "Naked and Afraid" might as well be the name of our era. Even so, we didn't see any of the 2016 presidential hopefuls wearing birthday suits. In a campaign full of surprises, astonishments, and shocks we were at least spared that.

No candidate went commando, no candidate went Goth, or gangsta, or—trendy though it may be—transgender. No candidate even went so far as trying to rock a skinny suit.

The 2016 election cycle has been a carny show. But the snake charmers, hoochie-coochie dancers, shills, hypes, and clip artists were as flamboyantly clad as Adlai Stevenson, Dwight Eisenhower, and Mamie. From a strictly sartorial point of view, it's been a dull and worthy campaign.

Or it has seemed to be. There are remarkable aspects to the candidates' unremarkable clothing. Their look is more interesting than it looks.

Start with the skinny suit's absence on the campaign trail. This shows that none of the candidates is actually stupid, whatever evidence we have to the contrary.

Diktat of fashion the skinny suit may be, but it's not a good look for people under six feet tall (Ben Carson, Marco Rubio, Rand Paul, Hillary Clinton) or with a body mass index in excess of 18.5 (Jeb Bush, Donald Trump, and Chris Christie, who, in a Thom Browne two-piece, could pop a waistband button outside the Trenton state house and break a window in Newark) or for anyone over the constitutionally required age to be president, and Bernie Sanders is double that.

A skinny suit is also wrong for people with big feet or wearing cowboy boots like Ted Cruz. In cropped pants with six-inch leg openings, Ted would look like he was stalking the corridors of power in cowhide water skis.

And one more reason not to wear a skinny suit is that Barack Obama can. The campaigns have been all about being different from President Obama. Some candidates said, "I'm more right-wing!" Some candidates said, "I'm more left-wing!" But every candidate has said, in the language of his or her clothing, "I'm dumpier!"

The slim chief executive with posture like he never lost the book that was balanced on his head at the Barbizon Modeling school wears everything well. He even got away with dad jeans. On him they made a "Like hell, I wear blue jeans" statement. Sometimes Obama makes the rest of us look like Oompa Loompas. As a result, sometimes he's been an unpopular president.

The best-dressed candidates of 2016 met fates that can—conservatively, as it were—be described as worse than unpopular. Rick Perry was just slightly too well turned out. His perfect tie knot was a rebuke to millions of men standing in front of bathroom mirrors every morning with a tangle of rep stripes reciting, "The rabbit pops out of the hole, jumps over the log, runs behind the tree . . ."

Perry's suits didn't wrinkle. Do we want a president with Secret Service agents packing concealed steam irons? And his high-fashion $400 Lafont eyeglass frames made him look like a sucker for the optometrist's cute millennial sales assistant. Real Republicans wear George Will peepers. Perry didn't make it past September.

Dr. Ben Carson was a front-runner for a while. Carson is a genius. We could tell by the way that his clothes showed he could plumb the deepest philosophical paradox: How can a man be so sharply dressed without going near the cutting edge?

In the end, however, the quietly luxurious and elegantly understated apparel of Dr. Carson made us all think, "Jesus Christ, how high is the doctor's bill going to *be*?"

Worst-dressed didn't work either. Rand Paul seemed to declare that libertarianism means the freedom to cut your own hair. His rumpled, preppy style was said not to project authority.

A preppy would disagree. Paul projected the authority of a boarding school housemaster who's thrown on something quickly in the middle of the night because the boys are up past curfew having a pillow fight. But most Republican primary voters did not go to prep school.

Someone needs to tell Jeb Bush that although traditional American business attire is called a "sack suit," this does not have to be taken literally. Jeb is the one fellow who should not have heeded the playground taunt, "Your mother dresses you funny," and gone home and let Barbara pick out his clothes. It worked for his brother and dad.

Chris Christie proved that the "portly man of fashion" has passed away. So long, Edward Prince of Wales, William Howard Taft, and Fats Domino. Maybe Christie's tough anti-immigrant stance scared off Omar the Tent-Maker. Christie had to get his suits from the guy who makes the tarps that cover boats in the driveways on the Jersey Shore.

The remaining also-rans may have made loud and clashing pronouncements, but their clothes weren't saying anything. And voters seemed to be listening to the clothes.

Ted Cruz took his sartorial cues from Rick Perry but seemed to think that he could avoid the pitfall of Perry's dandyism by ordering his clothes from Rochester Big & Tall. This might have worked if Cruz were big or tall.

Cruz was tweaked for wearing cowboy boots with a business suit. But that's standard practice for the good and great of Texas. Texans never know when they might have to rush out of their corner offices, cocktail parties, or fund-raising galas and go punch a cow.

Marco Rubio, likewise, was needled for wearing Cuban heels. But he's Cuban. And no taller than I am. I sympathize, though I wince at the thought of "Irish heels." (No shoes at all.)

Otherwise, Rubio was spruce without overdoing it, if maybe a little too given to tricolor coordinates and English spread collars that do not go with American chipmunk cheeks.

Dressed up, John Kasich was identical to every man in the Senate: "They'll never pick me out of the lineup." He wore dress shirts in white or, when he was pushing menswear boundaries, pale blue. His collars were plain and didn't spear-point or button or tab. If he's ever worn a pair of cuff links it was because they were a gift from President Reagan. His suits were custom-made to look as if they weren't. And his neckties split the difference perfectly between "quietly wealthy" and "Father's Day gift."

But, dressed down, Kasich broke out in the casual-Friday disease that afflicts all middle-aged American men. The symptoms are a pattern of stripes and bars crossing at right angles: "Dad Plaid," "Tartan of Clan Big Mac," "Slumberjack" pajama top.

This year's most abused candidate-casual garment was the half-zip sweater. I guess what it says is, "Look, I found a sweater that doesn't remind voters of Jimmy Carter or Cliff Huxtable." What I hear is, "I'm going to pinch my neck wattles in the zipper."

Every candidate who tried to look like a regular guy looked like a regular idiot. Regular guys don't run for president. We have our faults but that's not one of them.

The problem is dressing for the job. The plumber doesn't come to fix the sink wearing a tutu and toe shoes. We're deciding which candidates to hire. We're hiring them to lead the free world, not to play the sitcom buffoon next door.

We didn't always have this problem. It used to be that practically every adult male who wasn't in overalls or rags was dressed for the job of president.

Although, before the men's suit settled into recognizably modern form in about 1900, it was hard to discern what message any habiliment carried. No one is alive to tell us whether the mess of cravat around Thomas Jefferson's neck was a sign of debonair nonchalance or tied by a house slave who had strangulation on his mind.

Between 1900 and 1960, however, the message of every candidate's clothes was simply "man of substance." Any substance seemingly would do. You'd never know who was the puritanical egghead progressive and who was the reactionary happy-go-lucky ladies' man by looking at photographs of Woodrow Wilson and Warren Harding. And radical socialist Eugene V. Debs dressed like the other two guys until he donned prison stripes in 1918 for giving an antiwar speech during a war.

Variations were minor. There was a little too much tailoring on ex-haberdasher Harry Truman. Ike, a career military man, looked as though he was waiting for his dress uniform to come back from the cleaners. Adlai Stevenson, when running against Ike, was seen with a hole in the sole of his shoe. But this was taken by his supporters as a sign of just how serious Adlai was about putting a foot down on Republican shenanigans.

Dignity was so well preserved that Calvin Coolidge kept his while wearing a full ceremonial Sioux head-dress. He wasn't mugging for the camera, he was being adopted by the tribe. He'd recently signed the 1924 law making American Indians citizens. Coolidge's expression was as solemn as any Indian chief's, or as the suit and tie Coolidge wore for the occasion.

John F. Kennedy was perhaps the first politician to use his clothes as a sales tool. What he was selling was youth, or youth as it was conceived by the Greatest Generation when they were still youngish. He didn't wear a hat! This was tabloid news fifty-six years ago. He didn't wear a three-button suit. He wore a *two*-button suit. Oh, those zany Brooks Brothers! And Kennedy buttoned the suit buttons any way he damn well pleased, bottom button included. That's what a free spirit and breath of fresh air JFK was.

Richard Nixon, only four years older, had the dis-advantage of looking—especially during the candidates' first televised debate—dead.

Lyndon Johnson added a pepper dash of Texas with ten gallons on his head, the occasional jacket with rodeo yoke pocket flaps, and Lucchese boots (which are to working cowboy boots what John Lobb is to Thom McAn).

In the mid-1960s Texas had not yet blandly brought forth its Bushes, Perrys, and Cruzes. Texas was still con-sidered a slightly exotic and dangerous place. By the time LBJ got done being slightly exotic and dangerous even Nixon looked good.

Nixon looked like a grown-up, from a distance. Up close he looked like a grown-up reanimated by voodoo. He was so zoned out that he wore a suit and tie to go for a barefoot walk on a beach. But at least he was trying.

Trying to look like a grown-up is a fair description of all the presidents we've had since, until the awful thing that befell us in November.

There have been missteps. Gerald Ford was tempted by the skinny suit's evil opposite number, the 1970s wide-load. When would the manifest destiny of that lapel stop its westward expansion? Was it a necktie or was it a new board game?

The half-zip sweater is a badge of distinction compared with Jimmy Carter's cardigan. And what was Jimmy doing in Mister Rogers's closet?

Both Bushes did presidential well. The father sported a look that never went out of style because it never came in, while the son was modern enough to buy expensive suits but had them tailored to look like the 2 in a Jos. A. Bank 2-for-1 sale.

Ronald Reagan did presidential best. As an actor he was a pretty good politician, and his clothes were perfect. Central casting perfect. Technicolor perfect. Perfect beyond envy. You didn't want Reagan's clothes; you wanted a tub of buttered popcorn and a giant-sized soft drink.

Bill Clinton did not do presidential well. He had a "president's new clothes" problem. He didn't actually parade down the street nude like the emperor in the Hans Christian Andersen story. But there was always some kid (or journalist or Republican) in the crowd shouting, "He may not be naked now, but he and some bimbo had their clothes off a minute ago!" By the end of Clinton's impeachment trial it was impossible to look at him and not see Bill, at best, in nothing but his tighty whiteys.

Donald Trump, whatever else one may say about him, has had the sense to stay in his suit.

Trump, Sanders, and Clinton all have shown good clothing sense. Not good taste. They look like hell. They're not smartly dressed, but they're smart about dressing.

Trump's suits fit too badly to be an accident. They fit as if they're from his Donald J. Trump Signature Collection, priced from $155.87 and making you look like a hundred bucks.

But, according to Trump, his suits are made by Brioni, the venerable atelier in Rome known for fine fabrics, exquisite craftsmanship, and subtle panache. My sympathy to Brioni.

Trump's jacket waist has whatever is the opposite of a "tuck-in," maybe a "schmuck-in," because when he buttons his jacket there's room for another Trump inside. And when he unbuttons his jacket, it's like satin-lined worsted bedsheets flapping on a clothesline.

His shoulder pads are out somewhere past his clavicles, looking for the party. And good luck, because nobody has hosted shoulder pads like these since the 1980s.

Trump's French cuffs are not a protrusion; they're an invasion. They're Vichy cuffs.

Trump does wear good shoes—spit-shined (I'll make no cracks about establishment Republican bootlicking) lace-up brogues. Not slip-ons—TSA isn't an inconvenience to a man who never flies commercial.

The *New York Times* style section says Trump's ties are also from Brioni. Trump is six feet two inches and wears a Windsor knot, which takes up slack. How does he wind up with his tie hanging down like the tail of a scolded German shepherd? The ties must be made to special (and unwelcome) order. And the solid-color foulard was buried with Gianni Agnelli. Do the poor Brioni seamstresses have to go hold the ties next to fire trucks and highway construction cones to make sure the colors match?

Trump's supporters are proud that Donald doesn't listen to pundits, pollsters, special interests, or Washington insiders. Trump doesn't listen to his tailor either. Trump has perfected the "I-don't-listen" look.

And how does a self-proclaimed plutocrat get away with proclaiming himself a populist? By looking the way a poor guy would look if a plutocrat populist made the poor guy rich—so rich that he could have his own custom-made personal baseball cap to wear with his brand-new la-di-da Italian suit.

Trump's appearance—indeed, Trump's existence—is a little guy's idea of living large. A private plane! A swell joint in Florida! Lifetime membership in Hair Club for Men! Gold-plated showerheads! Gold-plated toilet handles! Gold-plated jumper cables in the trunk of the Cadillac!

Trump isn't a boiled-shirt, buttoned-up, unapproachable real rich person. Mitt Romney is a real rich person. Trump is a fantasy rich person—Rodney Dangerfield as Al Czervik in *Caddyshack*. When Trump's supporters see Trump they think, "That's me, in my dreams."

Trump wears a costume and Trump doesn't let himself be seen not wearing it. When he isn't in a suit he's in golf pants that announce, "They can't ban me from the club, I bought it."

Sanders is also intentionally, brilliantly, deaf to fashion. He wears mall cop shoes. He ignores the fact that on TV a button-down shirt makes your necktie look as if it has love handles. His suits are—nothing but a cliché will serve—all over him like a cheap suit. Where does he even get them? Does Sears still sell mail-order suits?

In photographs, one of Bernie's suits—he may have three—looks black. It can't be. Only chauffeurs and Brooklyn hipsters wear black suits. I'm not riding in the back if Bernie's driving. And, although he may be from Brooklyn and he may appeal to the hip, Bernie himself is about as with-it and happening as Leonid Brezhnev. But Sanders's campaign communications director Mike Casa has confirmed that the suit is black.

Bernie's style is as calculated as Trump's, and more cunning. Dressing like his voters was out of the question. Bernie doesn't have the tattoos for it. Besides, Bernie wants to lend adult authority to political ideas that might seem to have been cooked up in a dorm room bull session, which, a long, long time ago, they were.

You'd expect Bernie to go into lefty default mode—college poli-sci prof in tweed with elbow patches, cords, Hush Puppies, and a flannel shirt with a Rooster knit tie. But these togs would remind his supporters of homework. And socialism does entail difficult assignments such as getting past the border guards on the Berlin (or Oberlin) Wall.

It is, however, Bernie's good fortune to have fans so young that their parents are young, too. Those who Feel the Bern grew up in a world where even the minister at church was dressed in cargo shorts, Hawaiian shirt, and Tevas. Bernie bairns have hardly ever seen ITF—in the flesh—an adult in a suit and tie. So Bernie dresses like the only conventionally attired grown-up the kids have encountered—the funeral director when Grandpa died.

With Hillary's attire I confess I come to a sort of *Petticoat Junction* end of the line. I have difficulty decoding what her clothes are trying to tell us.

Men are famously bad at translating the language of women's clothing. We often wrongly think an outfit is saying, "Come hither," when in fact it's saying, "This may be a Starbucks in Youngstown, Ohio, but there's always a *chance* that Channing Tatum will walk in. Go away."

As senator and secretary of state Hillary Clinton maintained a regulation in-charge appearance, something like Angela Merkel's or Janet Yellen's, though she was less man-tailored than Angela and not as in-mourning-for-5 percent-GDP-growth as Janet.

But on the campaign trail Hillary's clothes became large and billowy, in hues that can be startling.

What she wears seems too big for her, though not in Trump's rich-slob way. There's something theatrical about what she wears, almost unstructured versions of David Byrne's huge suit in *Stop Making Sense*. (Incidentally, a good campaign slogan for most candidates this year.)

I tried to research the matter on the Internet. (If you think you've seen all the viscous bullshit a hard-fought election can produce, Google "Hillary's pantsuits.")

I did find out that a lot of Hillary's clothes are designed by Nina McLemore, who also makes clothes for Elizabeth Warren, Elena Kagan, and others with important jobs. The clothes are not cheap, but the prices aren't out in space on the Voyager mission with Brioni's.

I confessed my Hillary-ensemble illiteracy to a banker friend who doesn't wear Nina McLemore herself but who knows women who do.

The banker and her sources were complimentary:

"A serious person but with some conservative flair."

"Serious but not stodgy. And stylish but not sexy or inappropriate. Classic and classy but not Brooks Brothers' deadly dull pinstripes."

"She wants folks to see her as serious and put-together but not above them. The jacket/pants isn't a 'power' outfit. It's something all women wear and can relate to including those who don't go into a fancy office every day."

A lawyer said, "The colors are stunning and unforgettable."

Stunning, yes. Unforgettable, yes. But sometimes also visible only to bees. Bea Arthur? Susan B. Anthony? B-for-Bella Abzug? Hillary, those women aren't alive anymore. The young ladies who favor Bernie over you have never heard of them.

One comment indicated that, as suspected, the gene for common sense is carried on the X chromosome. "Nina fabrics pack magnificently and don't ever wrinkle." Wad up the other candidates and toss them on the floor, but do not try to fold, spindle, or mutilate Hillary.

Here is my version of the text of the prepared speech that Hillary's clothes give:

"We're being worn by a serious, professional, adult woman who's working hard—working hard to give off an amateur, lighthearted, youthful vibe. We aren't as sexless as a quilted housecoat or as inappropriate as a frilly baby doll underneath it. We're not stylish enough to be constantly 'borrowed' by Chelsea. And we're not stodgy enough to make you think Jehovah's Witnesses are knocking on your door. We're expensive but you can relate to us because we look like the designer outlet store didn't have us in size 8 so Hillary went with something roomier. Our owner isn't like that Carly Fiorina person, who may be bulimic. And you can stick us in a carry-on to go to Atlanta for your stepdaughter's bridal shower without worrying that we'll get smushed by the wedding gift Crock-Pot."

I assume choosing the right clothes was always part of successful politicking. But I'm not sure if clothing used to be so on-message.

We want our national leaders to be "seated and clothed and in their right minds." This and the possible future first gentleman bring us back to refuting Twain. People in the buff can have considerable influence on society. If the presidential candidates who attracted the most support appeared before us as they really are, without benefit of apparel, what we'd see is naked greed, naked ambition, and a naked old guy still sitting in a mud puddle at Woodstock.

# 18
# What They Stand for, and Can We Stand It? Part I

*The Campaign Platform of Bernie Sanders*

But enough of making fun of the candidates. Let us make unfun of them. If we're searching for a seriously unpleasant, annoying, and irksome way to view the candidates, we should look at their campaign platforms.

Yes, the campaign platforms are lies. But these are important lies. They reflect the candidates' interior monologues. The lies give us a picture of a candidate's self-image because the first person a candidate lies to is himself. Not to mention herself.

Bernie Sanders is a socialist. Of course every Democrat running for office for the past eighty-four years has been a socialist. They've all promised to take money from people who have more than they need and give it to people who are needy.

Democratic politicians care about poverty. As well they should, since poor people vote Democratic.

In 1966, at the height of Lyndon Johnson's "War on Poverty," the U.S. poverty rate was 14.7 percent and 28.5

million Americans were living in poverty. Now the U.S. poverty rate is 14.5 percent and 45 million Americans are living in poverty. Thus Democratic politicians care so much about poverty that—far from warring on it—they have become a kind of conservationist group, devoted to preserving it forever. Democrats are the Sierra Club of Poverty.

But Bernie Sanders is not merely a cynical political operative baiting the electorate with money and then switching money with food stamps. Bernie Sanders is a *real* socialist. Bernie doesn't just promise to take things from people. He thinks it's a sin not to. His faith demands stealing. If Bernie snatches a walker from a poor old lady he's doing a good deed. He's going to give that walker to an even poorer, even older lady. (I mean that strictly as a metaphor. If Bernie literally snatches a walker from an old lady, she'll snatch if back and beat him to a pulp.)

Bernie was never going to get the Democratic nomination for president. The Berlin Wall fell on his politics in 1989. But the old lady beating him to a pulp with her walker has grandkids. The grandkids don't know about 1989 because they weren't born yet. The grandkids support Bernie. Hillary wants them to vote for her. Bernie believes in stealing. The Clintons have sticky fingers. We'll see how much of Bernie's platform Hillary walks away with.

I visited Bernie's campaign website, went to "Issues," and clicked on "Income and Wealth Inequality." Here are thirteen kinds of stealing Bernie Sanders proposes:

1. *Make the wealthy "pay their fair share in taxes."*  Americans earning $100,000 or more pay

almost 78 percent of the federal income tax. Bernie's idea of taking a fair share of their income is the same as a shark's idea of taking a fair share of a surfer.

2. *Increase the federal minimum wage from $7.25 to $15 an hour.* There are 3.3 million U.S. jobs paying at or below the minimum wage. Multiply a $7.75 raise × 40 hours × 52 weeks × 3.3 million. Bernie will add $10,746,666,000 to the cost of providing jobs for unskilled workers. Assuming those jobs continue to exist. They won't. What robotics can't do away with self-service will. You'll be flipping your burger yourself at McDonald's and you'll have to bring your own *E. coli* to Chipotle.

3. *Invest $1 trillion in transportation infrastructure.* Boston's "Big Dig" comes to Fort Wayne, Indiana. The Central Artery/Tunnel project in Boston had an initial estimated cost of $2.8 billion. The final bill was $14.6 billion. It took fifteen years to complete.

4. *Reverse free trade agreements.* The one thing Bernie and Trump agree on besides the importance of acting like a jerk in public. Under NAFTA alone intraregional trade went from $290 billion in 1993 to $1.1 trillion in 2012. But Bernie wants that trillion to excavate an enormous leaky trench with an interstate running through it in the middle of Fort Wayne.

5. *"Invest" in a $5.5 billion "youth job program."* America has plenty of investors. They've already invested in creating 3.3 million jobs of the "youth job" type,

which pay at or below the minimum wage. Bernie
will have eliminated those jobs. So the 3.3 million
participants in Bernie's $5.5 billion youth job pro-
gram will each be making $16,667 a year digging
that Fort Wayne ditch.

6. *Enforce "pay equity" because "women earn
   just seventy-eight cents for every dollar a man
   earns."*    Give every woman a federally subsidized
   28 percent raise. Will this be retroactive and include
   Carly Fiorina's stint as CEO of Hewlett-Packard?

7. *Make college tuition free.*    And worth it.

8. *Lift the $250,000 Social Security tax income
   cap.*    Social Security's annual deficit is $39 bil-
   lion. About 2.5 million American households have
   income over $250,000. To put Social Security in
   the black Bernie will have to tax each high-income
   household $15.6 million a year.

9. *Single-payer government health care.*    Let me repeat
   something I've been saying for decades. (The way I
   usually repeat myself. Like Bernie—and Hillary and
   Donald—I'm old.) In 1993, when Hillary proposed
   universal free health care, I wrote an op-ed in the
   *Wall Street Journal* saying, "If you think health care's
   expensive now, wait until it's free."

10. *Mandate a total of fifteen weeks a year of paid family
    leave, sick days, and vacation.*    In most workplaces
    nothing gets done between Memorial Day and Labor
    Day or from the beginning of the Christmas shop-
    ping season, starting several weeks before Hallow-
    een, until the New Year's Eve hangover has abated

in mid-January. Then there's Super Bowl pregaming, winter doldrums, and March Madness devoted to filling out basketball brackets, followed by spring fever. Add Bernie's time-offs and there would have been one workday in 2016, and then only because it was a leap year.

11. *Universal child care for all children up to age five.*    Between this and free tuition we'll wave good-bye to our children in the delivery room and say hello to them again at college graduation. (Although we'll see a lot of them later because they will be broke and living in our basements.)

12. *"Make it easier for workers to join unions."*    Except there won't be any unions, because there won't be any workers, because there won't be any economic reason to hire them, because there won't be any economy.

13. And let's not even think about what Bernie means by *"Break up huge financial institutions."* Welcome to your new mortgage lender, 155th National Bank of Vermont, motto: "Cordwood Delivered, Snowmobile 4 Sale."

# 19
# What They Stand for, and Can We Stand It? Part II

*The Campaign Platform of Hillary Clinton,
the Crone in Crony Capitalism*

To people who believe in market capitalism, the Clintons are puzzling. They obviously aren't against making money. A Clinton speech costs like sin. Indeed, it costs more. CNN reports that Hillary and Bill collected $153 million in speaking fees between 2001 and 2015. Ken Starr, according to the Government Accounting Office, spent only $6.2 million preparing his case for the impeachment of the adulterous then-president. But the Clintons aren't capitalistic either. Putting aside a failed real-estate deal and a couple of cattle futures trades that seemed to require access to a time travel device, they've shown no entrepreneurial flair. Yet many successful bankers, hedge fund managers, and other titans of finance—who presumably believe in market capitalism themselves—support Hillary's campaign for president.

I suppose it all depends upon which market you're investing your capital in.

There will always be a bull market in political power and in being "friends of" the people who have it. The way to invest is . . . Well, Goldman Sachs didn't invite Hillary over to give its executives hair and makeup tips.

A lot of rich people support Hillary. A lot of rich people understand crony capitalism. Crony capitalists are like trust fund babies, except they made the baby by screwing the public.

Of course, you can't buy Hillary Clinton. You can only rent her. Being Too Big to Fail is expensive. This is why the practice of crony capitalism is limited to people who are rich already.

Meanwhile, for the rest of Hillary's supporters, her run for president isn't a real campaign. It's a bag of wishful thinking. An old bag of wishful thinking, if you will.

Hillary's supporters think that if they get another Clinton into the White House they'll get another "Clinton Era"—high economic growth, relatively peaceful world, some measure of bipartisan government cooperation, and a bunch of juicy scandals.

No doubt they'll get the scandals. But the 1990s Clinton Era was a legacy of twelve years of Ronald Reagan and George H. W. Bush. Hillary's legacy is eight years of Barack Obama. People think a Clinton is a lucky rabbit's foot. They forget that this rabbit's foot is attached to a dead rabbit—the Obama economy.

Hillary's campaign platform is so vague that it could have been concocted by my sixteen-year-old daughter. That is, reading Hillary's platform is like listening to my daughter when I ask where she's going on Saturday night. By the time I'm finished listening, I know less than when I started.

One thing, however, is clear. The platform is meant to be taken as a promise to bribe the least fortunate voters. To paraphrase the Wimpy character in E. C. Segar's *Popeye* cartoon, "I will gladly pay you Tuesday, November 8, for the fatty low-grade ground beef of your support today."

Hillary's campaign website is headed "A plan to raise American incomes" and begins, under the subhead, "Strong Growth" with, "Hillary will invest . . . "

This is another side to crony capitalism. Politicians never spend our tax money, they *invest* it. They've invested a lot of it. And they've been investing it for a long time. These must be very bad investments—or everybody in America would be rich by now.

"Hillary will invest in infrastructure, clean energy, and scientific . . . research to create jobs. . . ."

You can grow jobs in a petri dish?

"Infrastructure" could mean Bernie's Big Dig in the middle of Fort Wayne or it could be much worse—a six-lane 216-mile-long suspension bridge between Sag Harbor on Long Island where the Clintons like to fund-raise among Wall Street moguls and Martha's Vineyard where the Clintons like to... fund-raise among Wall Street moguls.

Clean energy? Maybe Hillary will re-fund Solyndra, the bankrupt company funded by the Obama stimulus plan to stick solar panels where the sun never shines.

Hillary doesn't pause to explain, forging ahead to "Provide tax relief for families."

Since Hillary has no plan to cut government spending, providing tax relief for some families means inflicting tax suffering on others. But never mind.

Hillary offers just two tax policy proposals. First, "a tax cut of up to $2,500 per student to deal with college costs." Great. That covers 15 percent of my daughter's tuition, assuming she goes to a public university in-state.

Second, "cutting taxes for businesses that share profits with their employees." Businesses already do that. It's called a payroll. And for Hillary's information—she being someone whose entire private sector experience was a couple of years at the Rose Law Firm specializing in *intellectual property in Arkansas* (italics added for my own amusement)—businesses have to meet that payroll whether they're making profits or not.

Next is "Unleash small business growth." Hillary will "expand access to capital, provide tax relief, cut red tape, and help small businesses bring their goods to new markets." When President Obama did that it was called Solyndra.

Then there's "Create a New College Compact"—$350 billion for state university tuitions. My daughter will be going to college for free after all! And it seems that she'll also get a government bonus when she's done because, according to the National Center for Education Statistics, total spending by all public institutions of higher learning is currently $310 billion.

Free college will save me $17,000, at the price of increasing my income tax by—let me take a wild guess here—$17,000.

Or maybe, somehow, college will still cost money. Because the next thing Hillary says is that she'll "Cut interest rates on student loans."

Like Bernie Sanders, Hillary can't understand why student loans have higher interest rates than mortgages or car loans. When did collateral become a hard concept to grasp? If my daughter doesn't repay her student loans will a repo man come and take back her Poststructuralist Phenomenology BA?

Hillary natters on.

She'll raise the minimum wage to $12. A bargain compared with the $15 Bernie Sanders wants us to pay the kid who, when we say, "Cheeseburger, fries, and a Coke," looks at us as if we'd asked him to recite the value of $\pi$ to the 15th decimal place.

Hillary will close the "'carried interest' loophole" that allows people who hedge the more risky kinds of investments (the kinds of investments that were made in, you know, crazy stuff like the Internet) to treat part of their income as capital gains.

It's not a "loophole," Hillary. It's in the Tax Code. It's a law. And you yourself have been known, when embarked upon the sea of law, to sail pretty close to the wind.

Then, when my eyes were glazing over and I was nearly lulled to sleep by Hillary's dull, predictable political subornation, the crony capitalism jumped up. The monster popped out of the box.

> "It's time to push back against the forces of 'quarterly capitalism' and boom and bust cycles on Wall Street . . . We need [to] . . . address the rising influence of the kinds of so-called 'activist' shareholders that focus on short-term profits . . . tackle dangerous risks in the financial sector . . . empower tough, independent regulators and prosecute individuals and firms. . . ."

Hillary is issuing a full-on manifesto for Central Planning—the very thing that, for a hundred years, has destroyed every economy where it's been tried.

Central Planning means giving *all* the power to government. And the head of that government will be Hillary.

Central planning is a crony capitalist's dream come true.

So, what a Hillary presidency comes down to is that you will do really well financially. You, that is, who donated enough to Hillary's presidential campaign.

# 20
# Paying for
# What We Can't Stand

Forbes *"Billionaires" Issue, March 1, 2016*

What would fulfilling the campaign promises of Hillary Clinton cost? Let alone fulfilling those of Bernie Sanders? There are a variety of ways to calculate the figures, all of which fall into the category of "laugh math." How long is a piece of string? The same length as the trail of digits that comes after the dollar sign in a promise of universal free health care. Medicare alone costs $600 billion a year. One third of that spending goes to cover end-of-life medical bills. This election is aging everyone in America. What would Medicare cost if the election's outcome makes us all sick to death?

The more exact answer to the question of how much money would be required to fulfill campaign promises is that there isn't that much money in the world.

On March 1, 2016, *Forbes* published its annual "Billionaires" issue, the definitive list of people who have all the money in the world. According to the magazine there are currently 1,810 billionaires. Their combined net worth is $6.5 trillion.

The proposed 2017 U.S. federal budget is $4.2 trillion. All the billionaires on earth put together could—if Washington is careful not to have any budget overruns—keep America going for eighteen months.

But we don't want the billionaires to do that. We want that money for ourselves. What candidates are really promising is, "I'm going to take the money away from rich people and give it to you if you vote for me."

Let's say there's a candidate who gets elected and does so.

If we take all the money away from every billionaire and divide that $6.5 trillion by the world's population of 7.125 billion, we each get a check for $912.28.

I just searched auto.com. You can get a 1998 Chevy Lumina with 180,000 miles for $999 in beige (although the door color does not seem to match the fender).

But everybody knows that all the money in the world really comes from America. Donald Trump has been telling us so.

Therefore the heck with 7.125 billion people. We'll take the $6.48 trillion and divide it among us 319 million Americans. We each get $20,313.48. That's more like it. If you've got a family of five (and, quick, adopt a few kids if you don't) we're talking 100 large.

We get $100,000.

Once.

Because now all the money is gone. And if any of the 1,810 impoverished former billionaires ever make any more money, I doubt they will let *Forbes*—or any candidates for president of the United States—know about it.

Also, we don't get our $100,000. We forgot to figure in "transaction costs." The expropriation of $6.5 trillion would require the establishment of an enormous, expensive legal and bureaucratic infrastructure. Billionaires have lawyers. The Justice Department is going to have to fight a lot of appeals court cases.

Plus, the army, the navy, the air force, and the marines would need to get involved. Only 540 of the billionaires live in the United States. There are countries that would defend their billionaires—so they could take the billionaires' money for themselves. Some nations are selfish that way.

And the billionaires themselves might fight back. The War on Terror has cost $1.7 trillion so far. I'm guessing that the world's billionaires, if they put their minds to it, could be four times as well-armed as fundamentalist nut jobs in Raqqah.

Furthermore, we didn't get our $100,000, because it doesn't exist. The world's 1,810 billionaires are worth $6.5 trillion *on paper*. They're not worth $6.5 trillion in gold, silver, diamonds, rubies, and pearls. It's not as if they have pieces of eight and Spanish doubloons stuffed under their mattress. (And a very lumpy mattress that would be.)

The wealth of billionaires is in negotiable assets—stocks, bonds, certificates of deposit, real estate, etc. The price of negotiable assets is . . . negotiable. It varies. (In fact, *Forbes* notes that because of market woes and currency fluctuations there are 221 fewer billionaires this year than there were in 2015.)

Dumping $6.5 trillion in negotiable assets on global markets would cause the markets to crash. The September 29, 2008, 778-point Dow slump erased $1.2 trillion in market value just on the New York Stock Exchange.

We could also examine the moral aspects of paying for campaign promises by taking away other people's money. Examining moral aspects seems like a ridiculous thing to do in this particular campaign season. But we could do it.

Did Warren Buffett (third-richest man in the world) come over to my house and snatch $912.28 from each member of my family? Good luck with my eighteen-year-old daughter, who's saving up for a pair of Manolo Blahnik high heels. She would have bonked Warren on the head with her iPhone.

Maybe the billionaires got rich by "exploiting the workers." Three of the *Forbes* list's six richest people created industries from scratch. There'd never been any workers in these industries because these industries didn't exist, making the workers in them hard to exploit because they weren't there.

The world's richest man pulled Microsoft out of his butt. All Bill Gates exploited was a line of 0s and 1s as long as a piece of string. Now Microsoft employs 118,000 people.

Number six on the rich list, Mark Zuckerberg, created Facebook out of less than that. All Mark had was a dumb idea that all the stupid people want to tell every stupid thing about their lives to all the other stupid people. Current net worth of the person with that dumb idea, $11.2 billion.

The world's second-richest person, Amancio Ortega, used to be an example of global poverty himself. He dropped out of school at fourteen to go to work to help feed his family. He founded his chain of Zara clothing stores by organizing thousands of poor Spanish women into sewing cooperatives. They're pretty well-off now. But they'd be even better off if they could divvy up Ortega's money. Which they can't because we need it here in America for universal free health care because we're all getting old and sick to death.

Maybe the billionaires got rich through "unfair business practices." Berkshire Hathaway is a company that's patient, prudent, and intelligent. Should we pass a law against that? To make things fair? What kind of legislation would make Warren Buffett hasty, impulsive, and idiotic?

Owners of brick-and-mortar retail outlets may criticize the Internet store Amazon.com for being unfair. But stores don't exist to benefit owners (even if Amazon *has* benefited Jeff Bezos to the extent of making him the world's fifth-richest person). Stores exist to benefit shoppers. And we love shopping on Amazon.

Would it be better for America to have my daughter drive seventy-five miles to Boston to buy her Manolo Blahniks and then come home and fall off her new high heels and drive seventy-five miles back to return them? You wouldn't think so if you'd ever seen my daughter drive.

And I suppose monopolistic accusations might be leveled against Mexican telecommunications magnate—and world's fourth-richest man—Carlos Slim. On the other hand, he brought working telephones to Mexico. Anybody who tried to make a phone call in that country before the 1990s can tell you it was like talking to the donkey, except you were less likely to get through. Will Donald Trump put an intercom in the Wall?

Of course, not every campaign promise is costly. Liberalizing immigration policy might even reduce costs. Or do better than that. With a liberalized immigration policy Carlos Slim will be able to come and stay in the United States legally. Then it will be easy to take his money.

# 21
# Another Attempt at Paying for What We Can't Stand

I have a plan to raise taxes. But this is a plan I think voters will support. I believe I have figured out a way to raise taxes that—for the first time in the history of taxation—will be fun.

Before I explain, let us take a moment to travel to another galaxy far away from the 2016 presidential election. Things are different here. Things are factual. Let us take a sample of fact and bring it back to earth with us: Our taxes are going up no matter what.

The American economy's two biggest problems are the federal deficit and the federal debt. We should fix those problems by cutting federal spending. But the Democrats are philosophically unwilling and politically unable to do that. It would turn them into Republicans. Meanwhile, the Republicans can't decide how to do it, or decide on much of anything else either, such as whether to shit or go blind. So the problems will have to be fixed by raising taxes.

Hillary is predictably liberal. She'll create more new government programs than you can shake a stick at; then she'll tax the stick.

Trump is predictably disingenuous. He claims he'll cut taxes, but he swears he won't touch entitlements. And he's full of governmental ideas as big and as ugly as his name on his buildings. These (buildings included, if he goes into bankruptcy again) will have to be paid for somehow.

Elect Hillary, and we'll get *obvious* higher taxes—on our incomes, investments, and businesses. Elect Trump, and we'll get *hidden* higher taxes—in the form of worthless U.S. dollars being printed to fund the deficit and debt.

Let's tax celebrities.

I don't mean we should tax individuals for being celebrated, as long as they're celebrated for something. Warren Buffett is celebrated for his investment savvy. He may think his taxes are too low. (He's said, "Even my secretary pays a higher tax rate than I do.") But I don't want to raise Buffett's taxes. Private investment benefits mankind by allocating resources to enterprises that— sometimes—succeed. (Notably different from govern- ment "investment," allocating resources to enterprises that don't—ever—succeed. The U.S. Postal Service, for instance. The Postal Service is, in theory, a "corporation." FedEx is, in fact, a corporation. Which would you rather own stock in? Sorry, the government has already bought you shares in the Postal Service. But I digress.)

And I don't want to tax celebrated athletes, artists, and entertainers even if they are obnoxious jerks and I'm not quite sure why they're celebrated. To me, most popular music sounds like angry potty mouths falling down a flight of stairs while carrying a drum set. But my daughter assures me that Jay Z is a genius. So I don't want to raise his taxes. Jay Z benefits . . . um . . . my daughter and her friends when they're having a noisy party.

What I want to tax is "celebrities"—that modern collection of fools' names and fools' faces, always seen in public places—who've never accomplished a thing and are famous for it.

The Kardashians are an example that's too obvious. But isn't "too obvious" the defining quality of what I'm talking about? The net worth of Kim, Kourtney, and Khloé Kardashian plus that of Kendall, Kylie, and Kris Jenner totals $300 million (at least according to the intrepid reporters at *Life & Style* magazine). I'd say a just and fair Kardashian tax rate (call it "IRS Form 7K") would be 100 percent. I'll let Used-to-Be-Bruce off the hook for having won a gold medal in the 1976 Olympic decathlon.

Taxing the Kardashians won't close the deficit gap. The budget deficit is $438 billion. This leaves us with $437.7 billion to go. But a 100 percent celebrity tax would apply to many other people. For tax purposes, my definition of celebrity is "Anyone who attracts or attempts to attract public notice by doing something requiring so little talent, skill, and sense that my kids could do it." With an extra 110 percent celebrity surtax when the celebrity attracts public attention by doing something that would get my kids grounded without TV, iPhone, or Internet until they're forty.

Johnny Knoxville and his *Jackass* crew come to mind. Not that they've been in the celebrity news much lately.

But I'm thinking about them because I spend half my day trying to prevent my twelve-year-old son, Buster, from doing the type of things that Knoxville and his buddies did—such as (and this is from an actual conversation that I overheard between Buster and his best friend Buzzy) taking a grocery cart to the top of the local ski hill and riding it down the terrain park. I don't even know where Buster gets these ideas. The MTV series *Jackass* was off the air before he was born.

Or the *Real Housewives* franchise. I'm sure my eighteen-year-old daughter has the *talent* to spend a fortune on clothes and makeup. I know she has the *skill* to throw the kind of tantrums that increase viewer ratings. And since she's legally an adult, she *could* marry a rich jerk and then act like Huma Abedin when she peeked at Anthony Weiner's Twitter account. But my daughter has too much sense for that.

I hope.

I also hope reality TV will be the first place where the celebrity tax is applied. And ex post facto for one particular reality TV show. On this show the proposed method of determining celebrity tax status was exhibited to near perfection. My kids are bossy. I've watched them use their allowances, and they possess the kind of business acumen that, if you gave them a license to mint money at an Atlantic City casino, they'd go bankrupt too. And they are adept at telling each other the sibling equivalent of "You're fired!"

If, by some chance—maybe due to a steep rise in the price of bullshit futures on the commodity market— Donald Trump turns out to be as rich as he says he is, we really could make a dent in the deficit.

And, speaking of a fool's name and face in public, there's a certain former secretary of state. From the "reset button" to smooth relations with Russia to the fruits of the flowering of the "Arab Spring," U.S. foreign policy under Hillary Clinton was . . . something my kids could do. (Or could if Buster were able to equip his toy drone with a bomb.)

When Hillary was a senator she introduced exactly three bills that became law. One bill created a National Historic Site in Troy, New York. One bill renamed a post office. And one bill designated a portion of U.S. Route 20A that runs through New York state as the "Timothy J. Russert Highway."

Also, remember how we were going to get a twofer deal when we elected Bill in 1992? What Bill's better half turned out to be best at was scrubbing the bimbo eruptions off the West Wing floors.

And Hillary's Whitewater deal made Donald Trump's handling of the Trump Taj Mahal look like a Warren Buffett investment.

Tax Clinton and Trump. He thinks he's rich. We know she is. The November election will take one of them to the White House. Before that happens, let's take them both to the cleaners.

# 22
# What They Stand for, and Can We Stand It? Part III

*The Campaign Platform of Donald Trump*

Donald Trump doesn't have a campaign platform. I assume, since he's running for president, that he needs one. Here are my suggestions:

## Declare the U.S. Government Bankrupt

The U.S.G. annual revenue is $3.3 trillion. Outlay is $3.8 trillion. Our national business is losing $500 billion a year.

An experienced chief executive such as Donald Trump would raffle this turkey.

And Trump (as previously mentioned) knows how—Chapter 11 filings for Trump Taj Mahal in 1991, Trump Plaza Hotel in 1992, Trump Hotels and Casino Resorts in 2004, and Trump Entertainment Resorts in 2009.

It's not failure; it's restructuring. And everybody wins. The U.S.G. has underlying assets with enormous income-producing potential.

For example, the federal government owns 640 million acres of land. Doing a little simple math, if we rent each acre for just $65 a month we'll be breaking even.

Only $65 a month for a whole acre! Surely a real-estate-deal-making maven like Donald Trump can convince people that that's really a tremendous, tremendous deal.

## Mr. Trump, Tear Down That Wall

We don't need a wall on our border; we need gates with turnstiles and ticket-takers. The right way to limit immigration (and make people in foreign countries pay for it) is to charge admission to the United States.

Disneyland costs $100 a day. There are at least 12 million illegal immigrants in America. By my calculation we're leaving $438 billion a year on the table. And America has many more attractions than Disneyland. (The S&P 500 roller coaster is much scarier than Space Mountain.) Plus, think what we could bring in from the food, toy, and souvenir concessions.

But what if people don't leave after we let them in? We'll ask Disney. Disney doesn't seem to have trouble clearing the theme park when it's closing time. (Maybe we should dress our Border Patrol differently. Nobody wants to run into a guy in a giant mouse suit in a dark alley in Mickey's Toontown.)

## Don't Make America the World's Policeman; Make America the World's Private Security Guard

And bill the world for it. According to the website small-business.costhelper.com, "An armed security guard typically costs $18–$25 per hour."

But the U.S. military has the best training and weapons in the world. Members of the U.S. armed forces are certainly worth double the going rate, $50 an hour at minimum.

There are 150,000 U.S. troops stationed overseas—$50 × 150,000 × 24 × 366 (this is a leap year) = $65.88 billion.

Foreign countries can pay up or go ask ISIS for help with their national defense.

## Expand the Brand

Trump may bill himself as a real-estate mogul, but his real genius is for branding. To date he's exercised his genius on only one brand, his own. But what a job he's done. There is, however, a brand that's even bigger than "Trump." It's "America."

All around the world people are imitating America—wearing blue jeans, listening to rock and roll and rap, tweeting, posting on Facebook, playing violent video games, binge-watching "Crazy Ex-Girlfriend," eating junk food, and becoming obese. We should be getting royalties for this.

I admit I'm fuzzy on the details. But Trump is the businessman, not me. BMI and ASCAP have made the royalty model work for American popular music. Since "White Christmas" was copyrighted by Irving Berlin in 1940, it has earned $36 million in worldwide royalties.

Imagine each American getting even a few pennies in licensing fees from 7.4 billion people every time any one of those people wears an ugly T-shirt, says "OK," or burns off his eyebrows lighting the BBQ grill.

## Speaking of TV,
## Bring Reality Television to Washington

Trump is good at branding, but what he's best at is playing himself on reality TV.

Washington is a perfect setting. The only competition is C-Span, which is like watching the canary molt.

All Trump has to do is do what he's doing already—let the cameras roll.

The genre offers endless possibilities:

*The Amazing Race* (we're in the midst of it)

*American Idol* (starring guess who)

*Snark Tank*

*Survivor* (Ted Cruz, as of mid-March 2016)

*The Bachelor* (Bill, when Hillary finally gets done with running for president)

*Keeping Up with the Congressionals*

*Project Runaway Government Expenditures*

*Eight Supreme Court Justices and Counting*

*Bush Dynasty* (canceled)

*The Biggest Loser* (see above)


## Eliminate Poverty
## While Saving Taxpayers $252.6 Billion a Year

(And, in fact, I'm serious about this platform plank.)

According to the U.S. House of Representatives Budget Committee, "There are at least 92 federal programs designed to help lower-income Americans." Together, these poverty programs cost $799 billion a year.

About 46.7 million Americans are living in poverty. The poverty threshold for an individual is $11,700 a year. If the federal government wrote 46.7 million checks for $11,700, the total would be $546.4 billion—$252.6 billion less than what's being spent now. And a family of four would get $46,800 a year.

Giving poor people money is a simple and straightforward way to eliminate poverty. But the government is spending 46 percent more money to eliminate poverty than it would cost to eliminate poverty by giving poor people money.

Bonus: Trump will get to shout his reality TV catchphrase at all the employees of ninety-two federal programs.

# 23
# Letter to Myself
# in 1968

Greetings.

(Sorry for the Selective Service joke, Pat. Don't worry; you'll flunk the draft physical.)

This is me (that is to say you) in the year 2016, writing to you (meaning me) back then in what you'd call now.

I (you) need your (my) help preventing a disaster forty-eight years in the future. If you think the politics in "Amerika" is a bummer in 1968, wait until you see 2016.

Unless you do something, a terrifying idiot is going to be president of the United States.

Otherwise, things have turned out pretty groovy. You're a little soft around the middle but still have your hair. Wife's a cool chick. (I'd tell you more about her, but she's currently in third grade.) The kids don't yell at you as much as you yell at Dad. You survived riding motorcycles. (When you take that hard right off High Street onto South Campus, some old bitch in an Oldsmobile is going to pull out in front of you.)

Yeah, you're a sixty-eight-year-old living in Squaresville, but mellow. (Wish I had that baggie of twenty-toke "Are-we-high-yet?" Mexican ditch weed. This twenty-first-century super-THC pot makes me paranoid, even though it's legal.)

But that's not what I'm writing to you about. You're a student activist (between tokes) and an antiwar protester. (I've still got the "Girls Say Yes to Guys Who Say No" button.)

You're hip to what's happening. Like the 1968 presidential race. You think LBJ's a bad trip? How would you like an LBJ in a skirt?

We've got one of those like groupies have crabs.

Incidentally, in a couple of days LBJ will tune in, turn on, and drop out. Drop out, anyway. For real.

"The Making of the President 1968" is about to turn uglier than a Mazola party in the DKE House basement passion pit on Sadie Hawkins Day.

Fat-ass, flap-jaw, party hack Hubert Humphrey; Gene "Roast a Weenie for Peace" McCarthy; and smooth operator, oh-*now*-you're-against-the-war Bobby Kennedy will be scamming for the Democratic nomination.

Trying to rip off the Republican nomination, there's the pig Nixon, the capitalist pig Nelson Rockefeller, and the pig who's blown his mind George Romney. ("When I came back from Vietnam, I'd just had the greatest brainwashing that anybody can get.")

The racist pig George Wallace will run as an independent on the Racist Pig Party ticket.

Come November, the result will be as bad as the time a few weeks ago when you swallowed that tab of STP.

How, you ask, can things in futuristic, ultramodern 2016 be worse?

Trust me. I am you. Trust yourself. Things are worse.

Dig this: a dude who's more of a capitalist pig than Nelson Rockefeller, exploiting the proletariat with a TV show dumber than Lawrence Welk's, who's got all the peace and love vibes of Richard Nixon and is a bigger racist pig than George Wallace.

That's the Republican front-runner.

Because . . . because the American public flipped out. Long story. You'll see when you get here.

And the Democratic front-runner is, as mentioned, Lyndon Johnson wearing a dress. (Actually, she wears a pantsuit. It's something a guy named Yves Saint Laurent invented in 1966, but you've never seen one. The coeds at Miami of Ohio aren't crazy.)

There are some other bad candidates.

There's one called Ted Cruz that you can't do anything about because he hasn't been born.

There's a black Barry Goldwater. Hard to get your head around. Anyway, he's pretty much out of the running.

However, there are also some candidates who are . . . well, they're bad too. But they're like "I Like Ike" bad. They're not heavy, freaky bad. They're squares. They're uptight. But they're regular. You know, like Dad.

And I really wish you hadn't yelled at Dad over Christmas break when he put up the "George Romney—Great for '68" yard sign. Dad turned out to be OK.

Anyway, your mission, should you chose to accept it (and, yes, that's still a popular culture catchphrase), is to make sure that neither Pantyhose-in-Cowboy-Boots nor the Pig from Uranus gets elected.

(Consult Issue 1 of *Wonder Wart-Hog, Hog of Steel*, winter 1967, "Wonder Wart-Hog Versus the Pigs from Uranus," by Gilbert Shelton for clues to the vulnerabilities of the latter. It's on the floor under your fringed suede vest.)

The reason I'm choosing you (us) is because we're about the same age as these jerks, which means that they are (were), like you are (I was), members of the "Youth Culture"—back when that meant something besides Botox. (Our wife will explain what Botox is later.)

In your day being young is a bond. It's membership in a private club. "Don't trust anyone over thirty." There's even a secret recognition hand signal. I still use it, without the index finger.

You can get next to these people.

The awful Republican is named Don Trump. He's a senior at Penn.

The awful Democrat is named Hillary (two l's) Rodham. She's a junior at Wellesley—exactly the same age as us.

It's possible we know Hillary already. She went to Maine East High in Park Ridge outside Chicago, right up Harlem Avenue from Oak Park where we went to high school. She was in a Methodist Youth Group. We were in a Methodist Youth Group. We may have *dated* her. And erased the memory.

So I have a plan. I've enclosed money. (No, you didn't get rich. A buck is only worth 15 cents in 2016.)

This Don Trump is the easy part. Skip some classes. I seem to recall you're ahead of me on that part of the plan. But (I checked our transcript) your grades are shit this semester no matter what. Fly youth-fare standby to Philadelphia.

Trump is the campus loudmouth New Yorker. You won't have trouble finding him. Tell him you're part of a commune that wants to pay too much rent for a crappy place in a bad part of town.

He'll be glad to have coffee or a mu tea or whatever with you. (You'll have to pay.) Slip the STP into his java. He'll freak. He's on the verge anyway. The cat's been a space case since birth. Skip town before he starts peaking.

*Way to go!*

I just checked the mental hospitals in New York. A "Donald Trump" has been an inpatient in the psychiatric ward at Bellevue since January 1968. Good karma, man.

Getting rid of Hillary Rodham is more complicated. First we need to have a little talk with ourselves about our politics.

Hillary Rodham—she's "Hillary Clinton" these days because she married. . . . What a long, strange trip it's been. . . . Oops, that Grateful Dead album won't be released for another two years. . . .

Hillary Rodham has a longer radioactive half-life than the Grateful Dead and half of them are—I regret to inform you—dead, gratefully or otherwise. But they're still packing venues. (Joke from the future: "What's the Grateful Dead fan say when he runs out of pot? '*What a shitty band.*'")

But I digress. We were talking politics. Hillary Rodham Clinton has only one serious opponent for the Democratic presidential nomination.

He's Bernie Sanders, a "New Left" type, and you *think* you agree with him.

Our politics will change over the years. Right now, you're under the impression that you're into communism. Like, "From each according to his ability, to each according to his need," says Marx. Far out. It's the monthly check from Dad.

Actually, a French socialist, Louis Blanc, said that. But, since you've never read even the CliffsNotes for *Das Kapital*, I won't hassle you.

Sometime in the 1970s you'll finally get a job. You'll be paid $150 a week. But when you get your first paycheck you'll find out you net $78.63 after deductions for federal, state, and city income tax; Social Security; union dues; pension fund contribution; etc.

And you'll say, "Wait, I'm a communist. I've protested for communism. I've demonstrated for communism. I've vandalized for communism. I've been tear-gassed for communism. And then I get a job with a big capitalist corporation and I find out *we've got communism already*. They just took half my paycheck! I'm not Nelson Rockefeller!"

Nonetheless, you and I continue to share basic political principles. As you put it to Dad at Christmas, "Get off my fucking case!"

This Bernie Sanders is on your case. Or he would be if you let him. He's six years older than we are and still hanging around campus, mostly at Goddard College in Vermont, which even you call "Flake Acres." He belonged to the Young People's Socialist League when he was at the University of Chicago. You know the type.

Bernie wants to "organize" you. If you aren't careful he'll talk you into going door-to-door trying to get "underprivileged" people to register for food stamps and vote. Since the underprivileged people in southern Ohio are rednecks with shotguns who're voting for George Wallace, you could get seriously shot.

When Bernie is rapping and you're stoned, he sounds like he's making sense, in a commie way. But he puts out bad vibrations. He's not a head. He doesn't smoke dope. But he's too smelly to be a narc. He's been married and divorced, and he's going to try to grope spaced-out Sunshine who's not wearing anything under her muumuu.

And Bernie "doesn't like" rock. He likes country music. Loretta Lynn singing "Don't Come Home a-Drinkin' (with Lovin' on Your Mind)."

It's the 1960s! That's where you're at. Meaning, Bernie doesn't like *Sgt. Pepper's Lonely Hearts Club Band* or *Their Satanic Majesties Request* or *Surrealistic Pillow*. Bernie doesn't like Jimi Hendrix.

If Bring-Down Bernie gets elected all of life will be like being trapped in a meeting of the Students for a Democratic Society writing the Port Huron Statement until the end of time.

He probably won't get elected. But that's only because of LBJ avatar reincarnation of Shiva the Destroyer Intercontinental Ballistic Sister Hillary Rodham.

You know that art major who chews her hair and thinks she's a witch? Hillary *is* a witch. Wait and see the spell she casts on this guy Bill she's going to marry who is the town dogcatcher in East Jesus, Arkansas, or something, and the next thing he knows he's a president of the United States who's being impeached for getting head. No shit.

Unless you make her chill out.

Wellesley is near Boston. Hillary's a grind. She'll be in the library. She wears a headband like our ten-year-old sister and the same big, ugly glasses as Mom. Has a favorite pair of bell-bottoms with weird (don't look at them on acid) stripes. Kind of cute but a major frowny-face. You'll spot her.

Wellesley's an all-girls school so you'll need an excuse to be there. Say you're an SDS organizer. Hillary's just starting to get lefty. Keep it platonic. (You'd know what that means if you'd done the reading for your philosophy survey course—"Deep Thinking for D Students").

Tell Hillary there's this lefty deep thinker she just *has to* meet. It's only 200 miles from Wellesley to Goddard. The two of you can hitch.

("Candidate Sanders: Hitchhiking should be legal, and made easier"—that's a newspaper headline four years from now when Bernie runs for governor of Vermont as a lefty deep thinker and comes in fourth in a three-man race.)

Hillary will *love* Bernie. She'll cop to his whole scene. She'll never become a Democratic Party bigwig working the levers and pulleys of power. She'll never be *The Man*.

She'll get stuck in Vermont, living in a yurt, chair-person of the Save the Snakes Coalition, one more old hippie burnout.

Bernie will ruin her life. He's already walked out on his marriage and he's about to get some other chick knocked up.

And she'll ruin his. Believe me, I have seen what Hillary can do to a guy. There's this poor dweeb Joe Biden . . . But that's another story.

Do your thing, young me. Let it all hang out.

And forty-eight years from now all we'll ever hear about Bernie and Hillary will be in the *Burlington Free Press* under the head "Domestic Dispute."

PS: If you can get some nude Polaroids of the two, slip them inside the dust jacket of *The Making of the President 1968* by Theodore H. White, on the poli-sci shelves at Miami's King Library. The book will come out in June 1969, and nobody has touched it since.

We'll pick up the photos at our forty-fifth reunion this fall—just in case.

Yours (as you will start calling yourself in two years),

P. J.

# 24
# A Better Way to Choose a President, Part II

*Ladies First*

$W$hat if we elect the president and then let the first lady (or, for that matter, the first gentleman) run the country?

Historical research and analysis suggest that allowing the role of head of state to devolve upon the marital partner or social helpmeet of the president would create a freer, stronger, more peaceful, and more prosperous United States of America.

**Martha Washington** is richer than George. She bribes the redcoats to bugger off back to England, saving us the bother of a Revolutionary War.

**Abigail Adams** is smarter than John. In her wisdom, she does not pass the Alien and Sedition Acts, which (to judge by the name of the things) cause America to be full of alien creatures such as Bernie Sanders's supporters who come from another planet and people (as the dictionary defines *sedition*) "who stir up discontent, resistance, or rebellion against the government and are named Donald Trump."

**Martha Skelton Jefferson** is dead before Thomas becomes president. Thus America gets its first black woman chief executive, **Sally Hemings**, in 1800. Hemings proclaims emancipation, passes equal rights legislation, wins the Civil War, and enforces Reconstruction—all with greatly reduced bloodshed and suffering because modern weaponry has not yet been invented and modern rednecks flying Confederate flags from their pickup trucks are still scattered in the backwoods looking for raccoons to wear on their heads.

**Dolley Madison's** diplomatic poise and social graces prevent the pointless war of 1812. The British, who've been invited to tea at the White House, do not burn it down.

While her husband James was ambassador to France **Elizabeth Monroe** rescued Thomas Paine and Lafayette's wife from the Reign of Terror. Therefore we may take it as a given that Elizabeth is a force with which to be reckoned. Her "Monroe Doctrine" tells Europeans to stop messing around in the western hemisphere *and* stop messing around in Europe.

**Louisa Adams** suffers from depression. She lets stay-at-home dad John Quincy take care of things like the household budget. He pays off the national debt, so there's plenty of money available for federally sponsored medical research. Prozac is invented in 1825. Washington has been a calmer and more cheerful place ever since.

Widower Andrew Jackson's niece **Emily Donelson** is too busy with Washington society squabbles (such as the "Petticoat Affair" over whether Secretary of War John Eaton's wife is a floozy) to sign the Indian Removal Act. Native Americans aren't caused untold suffering on the "Trail of Tears." And Emily also neglects to destroy the Second Bank of the United States. It issues "greenbacks," and green is her favorite color. There's no "Panic of 1837." America's first great depression never happens.

**Angelica Singleton Van Buren** fails to use her father-in-law Martin's influence with the New York state political machine to create the modern Democratic Party, thank goodness. Today Bill de Blasio is an obscure adjunct professor teaching "Sandinista Studies" at the New School for Social Research, and Rahm Emanuel is still running the meat slicer at Arby's.

**Anna Harrison** doesn't stand in the freezing rain giving the longest inaugural address ever and doesn't die thirty days later from pneumonia like her husband William Henry. And she doesn't, as Harrison's VP John Tyler did, annex Texas. Instead, Anna prudently waits for oil to be discovered so Texas can annex the United States.

Because Anna Harrison stayed out of the rain, John Tyler's wife, **Letitia Tyler**, an invalid, is never first lady and neither is Tyler's next wife, **Julia Tyler**, a silly rich girl.

Texas is so rich that instead of laying siege to the Alamo, Santa Anna starts "Occupy the Alamo," which, like all "Occupy" movements, is a complete flop. Lacking casus belli, **Sarah Polk** refrains from waging James K.'s war against Mexico. Therefore, today, the state of California is an illegal Mexican immigrant, and we get to deport it.

**Margaret Taylor** doesn't have much to do.

Ditto for **Abigail Fillmore**. And, thanks to the good work of Sally Hemings, Mrs. Millard F. needn't compromise her antislavery principles with the "Compromise of 1850."

**Jane Pierce** is reclusive. While in the White House she never comes downstairs. Since there is no Kansas-Nebraska Act or Fugitive Slave Act to be signed, she doesn't have any reason to come downstairs.

Bachelor James Buchanan's niece **Harriet Lane** is fashion-forward. The big event of the Lane administration is Harriet's lowering the neckline of her inaugural ball gown by two and a half inches.

**Mary Todd Lincoln** is a flake. But the nation doesn't need Abe, so who cares?

**Eliza Johnson** never comes downstairs either. So she can't get impeached. And because the House of Representatives never learns how to impeach anybody, history is spared Monica Lewinsky.

**Julia Grant** has no hard-drinking, poker-playing cronies to mar her administration with charges of corruption. The "Gilded Age" is so-called because it is a golden period of business probity, labor peace, and charitable concern for the poor.

**"Lemonade Lucy" Hayes** is a strict teetotaler. The hard-drinking Americans of the 1870s laugh off her attempt to impose national prohibition, and nobody ever tries that again.

**Lucretia Garfield** is safe in the ladies' waiting room of the Sixth Street Station in Washington while disappointed office seeker and would-be assassin Charles J. Guiteau is on the prowl. She completes a full term, as does her successor, **Mary Arthur McElroy**, the sister of widower Chester Alan Arthur. The most serious problem facing the nation is a budget surplus. So Lucretia and Mary go shopping.

Between 1885 and 1897 there are five first ladies. **Rose Cleveland**, Grover Cleveland's sister, is replaced when Grover marries **Frances Cleveland**, followed in office by **Caroline Harrison**, who dies in 1892, whereupon Benjamin Harrison's daughter **Mary Harrison McKee** takes over, after which Frances Cleveland returns to the White House.

Despite the rapid turnover, first lady policy remains consistent on the leading issue of the day, the gold standard. Gold makes lovely bracelets, rings, and necklaces.

Although Rose, Frances, Caroline, and Mary like silver too and consider it in better taste for tableware.

**Ida McKinley** is another invalid first lady. She simply doesn't have the energy and pep for a Spanish-American War. When unhinged anarchist (and Bernie Sanders voter *avant la lettre*) Leon Czolgosz *tries* to attack her, a nurse clobbers him with a bedpan.

Ida lives until 1907, allowing an orderly transition to the **Nellie Taft** administration, 1905–1913. Teddy Roosevelt, having charged up San Juan Hill with nobody there to stop him, just keeps going. Instead of "trust busting" Nellie institutes "trust bosoming."

**Ellen Wilson** is a talented painter. Like most artsy types she holds "advanced" opinions. Women get the vote right away. And, thanks to government medical research programs begun under Louisa Adams, Ellen doesn't die of kidney disease in 1914. She's around to heed peace protests and keep America out of World War I. She does not, however, establish the Federal Reserve. Banking "makes her head ache."

**Florence Harding** is a shrewd businesswoman. There's no Teapot Dome scandal. She already owns those oil-drilling rights, under her maiden name. And Florence instructs the Secret Service to "twenty-three-skidoo" Warren G.'s mistress Nan Britton. "And Warren, too, if necessary."

**Grace Coolidge** minds her own beeswax.

**Lou Hoover** is a cultivated and scholarly woman, a graduate of Stanford and fluent in Chinese. Her thorough understanding of economics and geopolitics sets the trend for cautious personal investments during America's "boring twenties."

One look at **Eleanor Roosevelt** changes Adolf Hitler's life—Pablo Picasso is a realist! Hitler embraces the "degenerate art" of *Les Demoiselles d'Avignon*, forgets about politics and hating Jews, and becomes a minor painter of the Munich expressionist school.

When North Korea invades South Korea in 1950, **Bess Truman** has her opera-singing daughter Margaret give a solo performance on the front lines and the North Koreans retreat.

**Mamie Eisenhower** and Nina Khrushchev bond over clothes shopping, leading to the 1950s signature dumpy-frock-and-babushka look and also to peaceful coexistence.

**Jackie Kennedy** provides a sharp contrast to Mamie. Jackie has exquisite taste. When she hears about something called a "Bay of Pigs" she vetoes it. "Honestly," she says, "I mean, perhaps a *Baie des Cochons*. . . . But, really, no."

**Lady Bird Johnson** undertakes a "Vietnam Beautification" program.

**Pat Nixon** suggests Dick take up a hobby, such as drinking. Henry Kissinger is unnecessary because of the enduring Mamie-Nina détente. **Betty Ford** goes to the Richard M. Nixon Center to dry out.

**Rosalynn Carter** gets all her policy advice from her ten-year-old daughter, Amy, who thinks "Stagflation" would be a swell name for a pony. It is, and, with a nationwide pony craze leading the way, the American economy begins to revive.

**Nancy Reagan**'s astrologer calculates that the nation (sun sign Cancer with Sagittarius rising) has its moon in Aquarius and Mars in Gemini. It's an auspicious moment. Nancy dresses up and gives a party for eight years.

Saddam Hussein's invasion of Kuwait makes **Barbara Bush** *mad*. And when Barbara gets mad . . . Hussein surrenders immediately. Ayatollah Khamenei and Hafiz al-Assad surrender too, just to be on the safe side. Yasir Arafat and Yitzhak Shamir also agree to do whatever Barbara tells them to. There is peace in the Middle East.

**Hillary Rodham**, an obscure real-estate developer and cattle futures trader from Little Rock, Arkansas, occupies the Oval Office for one term. She is little remembered today except for (thanks to the precedent set by Florence Harding) the shy, quiet, introverted devotion of her husband, Bill.

Meanwhile, with peace reigning in the Middle East, Osama bin Laden abandons his al-Qaeda start-up, goes into the family construction business, and dies in 2011 in the collapse of a shoddily built housing compound in Abbottabad, Pakistan.

**Laura Bush** perceives that America is facing a health-care crisis. She talks to hospitals, insurance companies, pharmaceutical manufacturers, and health-care providers and asks them if they can't, please, work something out. Laura is so nice, who can refuse?

With nothing to be irate about **Michelle Obama** devotes her full energy to making America fit. Average U.S. body mass index is now 18.5 and Chris Christie can do seventy-five push-ups, eighty sit-ups, and run two miles in thirteen minutes.

As for the 2016 election, with Melania Trump and Columba Bush out because they're naturalized citizens, the clear Republican front-runner is former Miami Dolphins cheerleader Jeanette Rubio, running on a platform of:

*GOP rules!*
*GOP rocks!*
*The Elephant's rolling!*
*Donkey's in for some knocks!*

Her expected Democratic counterpart is onetime interim provost of Goddard College Jane O'Meara Sanders, whose campaigning has been hindered because her super-PAC refuses to accept donations unless the money is organic, locally sourced, and GMO-free.

# 25
# The Last Damn
# National Political Convention
# I'll Ever Watch

*July 18–21, 2016*

In modern American politics presidential candidates are selected by primary and caucus voters during a process that lasts longer than the life span of an average house pet. By the time we're done listening to all that endless squeaking of the exercise wheel inside the smelly cage of politics we're ready to smother the gerbil and fall asleep.

The GOP convention in Cleveland was supposed to wake us up. We were promised a wild floor fight among deadlocked delegates and mass demonstrations in the streets outside.

You can go back to bed now. But I won't say, "Sweet dreams." Nothing that happened during the four-day Trump infomercial at Quicken Loans Arena changed anything about what's likely to happen in November.

Hillary "Lock-her-up!" Clinton should have a lock on the Oval Office.

The Republicans were playing sandman before the convention even started, when Trump announced that his vice presidential running mate would be Mike. . . .

Mike Tyson? That'd be exciting. Mike Myers? "Austin Powers, International Man of Mystery," could be useful in the election fight against "Mrs. Evil." Mike Huckabee? You're getting warmer.

No, it was Mike Pence. "Mike who?" ask all of you who live in the forty-nine states that aren't Indiana.

Hoosier governor Mike Pence is a Tea Party social conservative. He will attract to the Trump ballot all of the Tea Party social conservatives who were previously going to vote for Hillary. Their names are Bob and Jeanette. They live in Muncie.

## Convention Day 1

### *"Make America Safe Again"*

(Yes, but, at the same time, it might also be a good idea to "Make America Dangerous Again.")

The important thing that happened on Day 1 was a floor vote to pass the Republican Party platform. That platform contains a harebrained call to reinstate outdated Depression-era Glass-Steagall banking regulations, preventing banks from, basically, doing anything but provide checking accounts with personalized "decorative scene" checks, accept savings account deposits, make home loans, and get robbed.

Going back to the way banks were run when Bernie Sanders was a kid—brilliant! It will make things so much simpler. All we'll have to do is watch Jimmy Stewart in *It's a Wonderful Life* and we'll understand every aspect of the banking industry.

The other thing that happened was Donald Trump made an entrance to introduce his wife Melania. I mean *made an entrance*—with fog machines, Oscar ceremony lighting, and Queen's "We Are the Champions" blasting at sports event volume.

Do we want a presidential administration combining the features of disco, Hollywood, and the NFL?

Personally, as a New England Patriots fan, with Tom Brady suspended for the first four games, I was not so sure.

## Convention Day 2

### *"Make America Work Again"*

(Well, maybe, but if somebody would get interest rates and bond yields back up to normal the way they were when Jimmy Stewart was running the banks—I wouldn't mind retiring.)

The big news—in fact, as far as I could tell from checking the media, the only news—was that Donald Trump's wife Melania, in her speech to the Republican Convention on Day 1, parroted some things that Barack Obama's wife said in her speech to the Democratic Convention in 2008.

What poor soul, fresh out of journalism school, down in the bowels of some news organization, is forced to fact-check these things?

As if candidates' wives ever have *anything* to say at party conventions.

Here's a word-for-word comparison between the passages in question.

Mrs. Trump in 2016:

From a young age, my parents impressed on me the values that you work hard for what you want in life, that your word is your bond and you do what you say and keep your promise, that you treat people with respect.

Mrs. Obama in 2008:

Barack and I were raised with so many of the same values: that you work hard for what you want in life; that your word is your bond and you do what you say you're going to do; that you treat people with dignity and respect.

I'm sorry, but you can't plagiarize the content of another person's speech when the speech has no content.

If Melania had come out and said, "According to my husband, I should be very pretty to get what I want in life," that would have been news. Well, not news exactly, but candid enough to be newsworthy.

## Convention Day 3

### *"Make America First Again"*

(Not sure about this one. Smacks too much of the late 1930s "America First" pro-neutrality campaign that made us late for the game on Pearl Harbor Day.)

Ted Cruz refused to endorse Donald Trump. Cruz is like the wedding guest who jumps up on hearing the minister say, "If any man can show just cause why they may not be lawfully joined together let him now speak or forever hold his peace," and then mumbles something unintelligible.

I assume this was a pointless thing to do. But time will tell. Let's see how the marriage between Trump and the GOP works out.

Meanwhile, the anti-Trump street demonstrations were half-assed. Literally, in the case of this arrest as reported in the *Chicago Tribune*:

> Police Chief Calvin Williams said a protester whose pants caught fire got defensive when a police officer tried to put out the blaze. The man assaulted the officer, and "things escalated from there," Williams said.

### Convention Day 4

*"Make America One Again"*

(One what?)

The message of Trump's acceptance speech was that things are awful in this country and we need a Great Man to fix them.

Some of us more old-fashioned conservatives were looking around to see who that might be. Rudy Giuliani maybe? Rudy fixed a broke, broken, and dangerous New York City, and he preached a fire-and-brimstone sermon on Convention Day 1. But Rudy's getting a little scatty in his old age. Besides, it turns out Trump was referring to himself.

If he's going to win on a Great Man platform, Trump had better get to work. According to the opinion polls at the time of the convention, 59.1 percent of Americans don't think Trump is so great. Of course Hillary's disapproval rate is high too—55.9 percent. So Trump only has to be 3.2 percent great.

I suppose Trump could claim that he had 3.2 percent influence on how his daughter Ivanka was raised by his ex-wife.

Ivanka was great. She gave an excellent and polished speech invoking women's rights.

Which needed some invoking. Trump is favored by only 36 percent of women. Mitt Romney got 44 percent of the women's vote even though in 2012 my wife said, "Romney looks like everybody's first husband."

However, Ivanka's talking points could just as well have been presented at the Democratic National Convention. Maybe Trump should have ditched Pence and put Ivanka on his ticket for fear that Hillary would grab her for the Clinton VP slot.

## My Main Takeaway from the GOP Convention

I found it thoroughly refreshing. I'm wide-awake and raring to go. I should be. I just had a four-day nap.

# 26
# The Democratic National Political Convention

*July ?, 2016*

I kept my promise to myself.

# 27
# I Endorse Hillary

I endorse Hillary Clinton for president. She is the second-worst thing that could happen to America.

Dorothy and Toto's house fell on Hillary. I endorse her. Munchkins endorse her.

Donald Trump is a flying monkey. Except that what the flying monkeys have to say—"*oreoreoreo*"—makes more sense than Trump's pronouncements.

Better the she-ape of neo-Marxism than the flying monkeys' king on his 757, going to and fro in the earth, with gold-plated seat belt buckles, talking nativist, isolationist, mercantilist, bigoted, rude, vulgar, and obscene crap.

Better the devil you know than the devil who knows nothing. A devil who can't even figure out where the gates of hell are, and they've got his name right on them at Trump Tower.

I endorse Hillary. And all her pomps. And all her empty promises.

Hillary is wrong about everything. She is to politics and statecraft what Pope Urban VIII and the Inquisition were to Galileo. She thinks the sun revolves around *herself*.

But Trump Earth™ is flat. We'll sail over the edge. Here be monsters.

Hillary is a terrible *bien-pensant*, taking her opinions from the top of the social ladder she's been trying to climb since she was a teenager. In another time and place she'd be campaigning from Tara and with the slogan "Fiddle-Dee-Dee." Frankly, Hillary, I don't give a damn. I endorse you anyway.

Better *bien-pensant* than *pas de pensées*.

Better a nit of wit than a louse.

Better a mangy cat than a rabid dog.

Better the scurrying of mousy progressivism gnawing at the fabric of society in the White House than a rat on the Oval Office desk.

Better to root up the garden of free enterprise with the Democratic pig than run off a protectionist cliff with the Gadarene swine Republican.

Better a Scylla rock of a Clinton, which can be climbed and conquered, than a Charybdis whirlpool that takes us down the toilet with Trump.

Better to lay a sewer pipe that is Clinton than to lie in that sewer looking up to a reality TV star.

Better a Marie Antoinette of the left saying, "Let them eat fruit and fiber" than a *sans-culotte* in Madame Defarge drag who would be Robespierre if he could spell it.

Since Athens in the fifth century BC the worst enemy of democracy has been the demagogue. But—O tempora! O mores!—now we've got a firebrand soapbox orator who cannot so much as put a coherent sentence together. He likes to "talk bigly."

Here's to you, Hillary, for saving your best bloviation for your highly paid speeches to shady bankers. I would, if I could, pay Trump more to shut up.

Hillary, I choose you, Goldman Sachs's milch cow, over the Cretan Bull siring his herds of mini-Minotaurs—half-men, half-bullshit—laying waste to the country.

Hillary, you are as bad as Grendel in *Beowulf* but still not as bad as that Grendel's mother of a Donald Trump.

Hillary, for instance, is not as bad a real-estate developer as Trump.

Trump casinos, Trump hotels, and Trump resort bankruptcies cost lenders and investors nearly $4.5 billion. The $39.2 million that Hillary cost taxpayers for the investigation of her Whitewater scam is nothing by comparison.

True, Hillary screwed up during the attack on the U.S. consulate in Benghazi. As opposed to Donald Trump, who would have sent his supporters to boo and hiss the Islamic extremist attackers and then ask Libyan police to take the extremists away.

Yes, Hillary sent top-secret State Department documents to her personal e-mail server. But this shows that she can keep a secret, even if she doesn't know where to put it and it ends up decorating her Pinterest site. Trump would have branded the documents as "Trump Top Secrets" and sold them on eBay.

Also, at least the CIA and NSA *tell* Hillary secrets. Would you tell a secret to Donald Trump?

Speaking of which . . . Like a toddler in a home with a loaded handgun, sooner or later Donald will find the place where the grown-ups hid "the button." To avoid messy mushroom-shaped incidents, better lock the thing in a safe. Set the combination to "411." He'll never think of that. Donald hates information.

Hillary, I endorse you although you don't belong in power—you picture of self-satisfaction out of doors. Count yourself a Desdemona and me the Iago of your fans, you ding-dong bell in your West Wing, wildcat in your can't-stand-the-heat-get-out-of-the-kitchen, plaster saint in your martyrdoms, player in your housewifery, and housewife in your bed. (Sorry, my mistake: That's somebody else's wife in bed with your husband.)

*You're a smug one, Hillary,*
*You really are a snoot,*
*You're as cuddly as a cactus, you're as charming as a*
    *newt, Hillary,*
*You're a bad banana in a garish and expensive power suit!*

*You're a limousine liberal, Hillary,*
*Your heart's an empty hole,*
*Your brain is full of Sidney Blumenthal, you have boiled*
    *kale in your soul, Hillary,*
*I endorse you with a thirty-nine-and-a-half-foot pole!*

In sure and certain hope of resurrection I endorse Hillary.

She'll work a miracle for the Republican Party. I've seen the GOP die and be buried before—with Richard Nixon, Gerald Ford, and Watergate. In four short years there was a Second Coming.

I endorse Hillary.
*Ecce feminae.*
Behold Jimmy Carter in a pantsuit.

(*Postscript:* I guess my endorsement didn't carry much weight with blue-collar voters in crucial swing states.)

# 28
# The Nowhere Leadership
# Is Headed To

America is experiencing a change in the nature of leadership. We're getting rid of our leaders. And we're starting at the top.

Many people offered themselves as candidates for president in 2016. They shared a number of traits: limited ideas, unimaginative policy positions, minimal charisma, and prior accomplishments in statecraft ranging from modest to none.

They were all inept politically. One heavily publicized hopeful was haunted by "ghost politics"—his ideology having been killed when the Berlin Wall fell on it. The noisiest front-runner had hardly any politics. His chief contender had nothing but. She was infested with politics to the point where her every act and action became political, like a cat so badly plagued by fleas that it cannot eat or sleep and scratches itself bald.

Nearly a score of these partial or complete nonentities were taken seriously as presidential candidates. Eight or ten were, at one time or another, strong contenders in the opinion polls. Not one could be plausibly imagined as president of the United States.

Survey the field of candidates and think about childhood games of follow-the-leader. These are the kids we were trying to lose.

Chris Christie is the bully who failed. He would have gotten together with his friends and taken your lunch money, if he'd had friends.

Marco Rubio doesn't look old enough to drive. He steered his campaign like a sixth-grader who could either see over the dashboard or reach the pedals but not both at the same time.

Ted Cruz is the earnest, fervid boy speaking in tongues at the tent revival while his pals sneak around the back to smoke cigarettes, drink moonshine, and smooch with Sunday school girls.

The more adult candidates did not evoke adulthood in any way that we'd care to have youngsters imitate.

Ben Carson is the slightly dotty uncle who dresses in a monogrammed blazer, ascot, and velvet slippers to wash his car.

Every family business has a Jeb Bush, one of the founder's grown kids that nobody knows what to do with. Make him president of that useless subsidiary in the District of Columbia?

Bernie Sanders is a member of an amateur theatrical troupe playing Santa Claus against type—grumpy, skinny, clean-shaven, and promising to give you presents *especially* if you've been naughty.

Hillary Clinton is the sum of all fears about liberalism's strategy for doing well by doing good. She's also Lucy with Charlie Brown's football.

John Kasich just barely manages to be *gubernatorial*.
And Donald Trump . . .

Donald Trump is the fellow who sells you the over-
priced luxury co-op on Pennsylvania Avenue. He is not
the person who you, as a member of the co-op board,
chose as a resident.


If America didn't want a poor choice of leaders, America
wouldn't have a poor choice of leaders.

We're a democratic country, free to make our own
decisions, and we have strong personal feelings about
our decision-making. That's the problem.

"Don't take this personally" is good advice, especially
in a political system based on the rule of law and not of
persons. But selecting the president has become increas-
ingly personal.

We used to vote for people we admired. Admiration
is best done from far away. William McKinley conducted
his entire 1896 presidential campaign by sitting on the
front porch of his house in Canton, Ohio, a place that's
far away from most things.

And McKinley was admirable. He was honest. He
supported a sound dollar and fair treatment of labor. He
was a devoted husband to his invalid wife.

But admiration has its disappointments.

Voters admired the brilliance of Woodrow Wilson. He'd
been president of a college everyone had heard of back
when going to college was an unheard-of thing. Surely he
was smart enough to keep the world war a world away.

Coolidge was admirably calm, the eye of the Roar-
ing Twenties storm. But pouring oil on troubled water

works only in metaphors and probably pollutes the environment.

Hoover was a great technocrat, the admired engineer tending the great steam engine of American economic growth, which exploded.

On close inspection all feet are clay. The march of leadership was tracking dirt across the national carpet. We were personally disappointed in our leaders.

Meanwhile, the expansion of mass media in the twentieth century made it hard for the leaders to keep their distance from the led. We, personally, knew too much about them.

Leadership became a personal matter. Therefore it made sense to abandon hero worship and pick leaders on a personal basis, because we like them. The trend is evident as far back as Warren Harding, who was nothing if not—and nothing other than—affable.

Franklin Roosevelt was a ruthless politician who knew how to cozy up for fireside chats, the wolf feigning kitten on our hearth. Don't let on that Grandma voted for Willkie.

Harry Truman was everybody's poker buddy while Thomas E. Dewey, a former prosecutor, would have called our bluff when we bet on a pair of fours.

"I Like Ike" was the nonpareil campaign slogan. The best Adlai Stevenson could do was "We Need Adlai Badly," and badly was how his campaign went. From then until this year the more likable presidential candidate has usually won.

Exceptions came only in exceptional circumstances. Dreadful Richard Nixon ran in the throes of a lost war and then against mooncalf George McGovern. The grating

Jimmy Carter was selected from a field of political debris left behind by Washington's worst political scandal.

Otherwise, Jack Kennedy's wink defeated Nixon's glare. Rowdy cowboy LBJ prevailed over stern, scary Goldwater. Reagan raised a toast of good cheer while Carter and Mondale offered a jar of pickles. Bush was a day at the Kennebunkport beach; Dukakis was a month of homework.

Bush invited us to a Republican party; Clinton held a kegger. George W.'s frat boy antics (and friendly Supreme Court) held more appeal than a man who, himself, joked that the Secret Service code name for Al Gore was "Al Gore." John Kerry lost us when he ordered Swiss on a Philly cheese steak. And with Barack Obama, first the hope beat cranky John McCain, then the change beat the folding money of a boring old rich guy.

But amiability can be as tenuous as admirability. Mass media made admirable leaders disappear. Now the mass media have New Media stepchildren—twenty-four-hour cable news, the Internet, Twitter. New Media make amiable leaders hard to like.

We've now learned everyone's dark secrets. Our leaders don't turn out to be likable after all.

Kennedy was a philanderer. Johnson was too and a monomaniac besides. Distant and chilly parent Ronald Reagan concealed his slide into senility. Bush 41 was so out of touch that he was astonished by the workings of a grocery store checkout counter.

We know more about Bill Clinton's sexual peccadilloes than we can, if we're of a certain age, remember about our own. W. pranked us into going to war. And while we may still like Obama he doesn't like us. The look of disappointment rarely leaves his face. When he goes on TV we know we'll get scolded.

Leadership has become more personal yet. We're not satisfied with liking our leaders. We want the truth. We want to know them as humans. We want our leaders to be authentic.

And we've succeeded. All our 2016 presidential candidates were authentically human, which is to say deeply flawed.

The number of candidates was gradually winnowed down to five, with the skeletons from their closets on full display. (In one case, proudly.) To my knowledge the word "likable" was never used in connection with four of them. The one candidate who could be so described—John Kasich—was, and would remain, in last place.

Admirable leaders may not display the virtues we expected. Amiable leaders may not be the friendly guides we sought. But now we seem intent on electing a leader we neither look up to nor like.

Therefore we will elect someone with no means to lead us.

And we did.

# 29
# The Campaign Trail
# of Sneers

No two candidates for the American presidency have ever faced such formidable opponents. It would have been a tough race if they had been running against each other. But they weren't. They were running against themselves.

It is astonishing that Donald Trump managed to eke out a victory over Donald Trump at the polls. It is amazing how narrow the margin was by which Hillary Clinton defeated Hillary Clinton.

## How Did They Do It?

That Trump won is ridiculous. And ridiculousness is a part of the explanation. Every comic genius in the country brilliantly ridiculed, derided, mocked, and taunted the very idea of a Trump presidency. Voters who entertained that very idea, or who were even slightly tempted to entertain it, took note and responded with the kind of mild deference that objects of ridicule, derision, mockery, and taunts usually display. This did wonders for Trump.

The amount of outrage directed at Trump helped too. There seemed to be an inexhaustible reserve of outrage. It was used unsparingly. Then Trump insulted the heroism of John McCain. Then Trump heaped contempt on the grief of Gold Star parents Khizr and Ghazala Khan. Then Trump opened his heart to Billy Bush. More and more and more outrage was needed. In the end, the demand outstripped the supply.

The news media also made a mistake in the way it went about trying to understand Donald Trump. This was not any one of the mistakes that the news media, endlessly since the election, has been copping pleas to and shouting *mea culpas* about. The mistake was not "living in a bicoastal bubble" or "failure to comprehend white working-class discontents" or "excessive reliance on faulty polling data." The mistake was not watching *The Apprentice*.

People who work in the news media do not watch *The Apprentice*. This is not because we're elites or snobs, much less because we're too smart to watch reality TV—we're the news media; we're so stupid that we watch C-SPAN. People who work in the news media do not watch *The Apprentice* because of what's been happening in the news media for a number of years, causing all of us who work in it to never want to hear the words "You're fired" again.

This was a mistake. Donald Trump, the actor who plays "Donald Trump," appeared on *The Apprentice* for eleven years. At its peak, the show had 20 million viewers. And Trump is a good actor. Donald Trump is almost as good as Alec Baldwin at being Donald Trump.

Trump played the boss you wish you had. Not the boss you wish you had *at work*. He's the boss you wish you had *after work,* when you're having drinks with your coworkers and telling hilarious stories. "You won't believe what that buttwad did today!"

But there's another side to this character. From time to time on the show "Trump" drops the fuss and bluster and holds forth with his business philosophy. The change is shocking. The advice given by the caricature bully comes straight off the motivational posters on the break room wall. Stuff like:

*If Opportunity Doesn't Knock Get a Doorbell*

*Don't Chase Your Dream, Wake Up*

*There Is No "Me" In "Team" Unless You Spell It Backwards and Leave Out the T&A*

I made those up due to not being able to stand watching more than about two and a half episodes of *The Apprentice.* But I was taking notes, and I honestly did hear Trump say, "Strike a balance between practicality and creativity," and, "Get the best people—and watch them."

So here was Trump the atavistic throwback being Trump the font of current wisdom. The Trump character on *The Apprentice* managed to come across as Archie Bunker and Meathead rolled into one.

## But How Did *She* Do It?

"Don't put all your deplorables in one basket" is advice that comes too late. What Hillary supporters lacked in good counsel, they've been trying to make up for with good excuses.

There's the F.B.I. excuse. But it's not like Hillary's e-mail scandal hadn't been front and center throughout the campaign. And F.B.I. director James Comey let Hillary off the hook—again—four days before the election. What Comey *can* be blamed for was putting the spotlight on Hillary aide, spooky-ooky lost-member-of-the-Addams Family Huma Abedin, and on Abedin's obviously insane estranged husband, Anthony Weiner.

Voters were thereby given a timely reminder of just how icky things get in the Clinton inner circle. This, however, does not account for Hillary's loss. The icki-est reminder of all, Bill, had also been front and center throughout the campaign.

There's the "glass ceiling" excuse: Americans are just too backward to elect a woman. But people all over the world—some at least as backward as Americans—have elected women.

Angela Merkel runs Germany. Theresa May runs Britain and Margaret Thatcher used to. Aung San Suu Kyi runs Burma. Then there was Golda Meir in Israel and Indira Gandhi in India. Mrs. Gandhi was first elected in 1966, at a time and in a place that—no matter what your yogi at the ashram says—was more sexist than present-day America.

And there's the "whitelash" excuse: Trump was elected by grumpy old white guys and nobody but grumpy old white guys. This doesn't add up. I've done the math. In the three generations of my immediate family there are nine people, and only a third of us qualify as grumpy old white guys, and one of us has been dead for years.

It would be more honest to admit that Hillary is boring, stupendously boring. She has a positive genius for being dull. She could be giving away puppies to six-year-olds and the kids would be pulling at their parents' sleeves whining to leave.

There's an automaton quality to the tediousness of Hillary. This was on full display at the "Commander-in-Chief Forum" on September 7, 2016, where Clinton and Trump made back-to-back appearances hosted by Matt Lauer, who was himself mechanical and repetitious.

Yet to call Hillary robotic is an insult to androids. She's more like someone trapped inside a Hillary costume, one of those dressed-up characters pestering tourists in Times Square. If you peer at the mask you can see her little, panicked, furtive eyes darting around inside the eyeholes. "Get me out of here!" And get her out of there is what the Democrats should have done.

Meanwhile, Trump was the guy from the mailroom who somehow wound up with a job interview for the position of National Sales Manager. If you promote him it will be a disaster. But if you leave him in the mailroom he'll take his pants down, sit on the Xerox machine, and fax the result to all your customers.

On Monday, September 26, 2016, Clinton and Trump met for their first head-to-head debate. What was the evening's big news? Deion Jones returned a 90-yard interception to score a touchdown and cap the Atlanta Falcons' victory over the New Orleans Saints, 45-32.

I didn't get to see it. I was watching the presidential debate—so you didn't have to.

Watching the debate was as interesting as watching cow flop bingo at the county fair. Trump tried to paint a detailed picture of what's wrong with America using a mop for a brush. Clinton was good on the details—too good. Details were all she had. Lots and lots of highly detailed little thises and thats, as if furnishing the White House for dolls is her plan.

And she kept saying, "I have a plan." As a phrase that sets off alarm bells, "I have a plan" is right up there with "Hold my beer and watch this!"

Hillary had the best riposte. She brought up the notion that Donald is someone who shouldn't be allowed anywhere near nuclear weapons.

Trump: "That's getting old."

Clinton: "But good."

And Trump had the best line: "Hillary has experience, but it's bad experience."

Who won the debate? Whomever you wanted. It was Soviet bloc judges scoring Olympic gymnastic events during the Cold War. Sixty-two percent of respondents to CNN's instant polling said Clinton won. Eighty-two percent of respondents to the *Drudge Report*'s instant polling said Trump did.

And yet the debate was highly informative—*if you turned the sound off.*

The event was broadcast with a split screen so that each presidential candidate was visible while the other candidate was talking. The talk was insipid, but the expressions on the candidates' faces were fascinating.

Trump was serious of mien. He concentrated intently on what Hillary was saying. Sometimes there was a little twitch of annoyance; sometimes, a small frown of disagreement. But mostly he looked deeply thoughtful.

(Where he got that look is anyone's guess. Maybe he purchased it at the same strange haberdashery where Hillary buys her Hillary costume.)

Clinton is supposed to be the one with the deep thoughts. But there she was thoughtlessly making rude grimaces whenever Trump was speaking.

Mom always said, "You shouldn't make faces—your face may get stuck that way." Hillary's face got stuck that way.

She spent the whole evening with a wipe-that-look-off-your-face look on her face. She smirked. She sneered. She radiated smugness.

The election may have been won by Trump, but it was lost by the smug look worn by Clinton and everyone in the Clinton camp.

And *everyone* was in the Clinton camp—every sanctimonious celebrity, preachy egghead, public Goody Two-shoes, plaster-saint pundit, simon-pure editorial writer, and mealy-mouthed business bigwig. The Clinton campaign was a Who's Who of the self-righteous and a what's-what for the holier-than-thou.

Hillary repeatedly mugged for the camera with a ham actor's pantomime "gasp of disbelief." Except, unlike Donald, she's not a good actor, and her expression came off looking like an ad for cheap dentures.

Hillary indulged in nasty smiles of condescension. She adopted a pout that said, "What's a smarty like me doing with a dummy like him?" She had an air about her that suggested she just couldn't believe that somehow, oh my gosh, she'd been dragged up on stage to debate a talking dog.

It bit her.

## The Campaign Grinds On

As it was with *The Apprentice*, so it was with the presidential campaign. I could watch only so much of it, and, after the first debate, I didn't try very hard.

I did note that the campaign quickly sunk to the level of the "Food fight!" scene in the movie *Animal House*. Except not funny. We *wished* we had a candidate with as serious and intelligent a statement to make as John Belushi did when he stuffed his mouth with cottage cheese, pressed on both cheeks, and said, "I'm a zit."

But it's too late now (in several ways) to nominate John.

Mostly I wondered, "What are these people doing running for president *at my age*?" I'm a few months younger than Hillary and a year younger than Donald. During the campaign I had flown from Boston to Chicago. That's all I'd done. I drove to Boston, got on a plane, flew to Chicago, and took a cab to my hotel. *I was exhausted.* I needed a stiff drink, a leisurely dinner, a nightcap, and I was in bed by nine p.m. watching CNN, where I saw the candidates arriving at the eighth or tenth event they had scheduled that day.

Something is wrong with these people. And something is wrong with the rest of us. Why have we turned running for president into the Boston Marathon, complete with the Internet as the Tsarnaev brothers?

I did enjoy the campaign's exquisite ironies. America was having a "Latin American Moment"—and Latinos had nothing to do with it. American voters seemed to be looking for a South American *caudillo* strongman-style leader. But Trump, with xenophobic flair, did everything he could to avoid getting Hispanic votes. And the two primary candidates with Hispanic backgrounds couldn't have been more *norteamericano* in their politics.

There was a terrible outbreak of "mansplaining" on the campaign trail—all of it done by a woman. Hillary Clinton was the person with the patronizing and prolix explications.

That American politics is controlled by big-money campaign donors turns out to be a myth. Charles and David Koch had about as much influence on the selection of candidates and the outcome of the election as the National Pork Producers Council has on Middle East peace negotiations.

Bernie Sanders built a formidable campaign machine funded by supporters who contributed their tie-dyed head hankies, used hacky sacks, and the stems and seeds from the bottom of their medical marijuana prescription baggies.

Donald Trump got most of his campaigning done on the cheap by making a public spectacle of himself. He set his pants on fire knowing that reporters and camera crews would have to cover the blaze.

Hillary Clinton did have the traditional big-bucks-backers. But she didn't need them. She could have gotten to exactly where she wound up, for free, by tweeting everything that's on YouTube about Donald Trump.

Which shows how all all-important major media isn't. Watching major media during the 2016 presidential campaign was like turning on the Weather Channel to see what was happing with Hurricane Matthew and finding the forecasters talking about nothing but how great the big-wave surfing conditions were off the coast of South Carolina.

## Meanwhile, at Libertarian Party Presidential Campaign Headquarters

Let's not forget the Libertarian Party. Okay, let's forget the Libertarian Party.

The Libertarians didn't make the kind of impact that you'd expect in an election where the two main-party candidates seemed to be locked in a struggle to see who could get "unfriended" most on Facebook.

Gary Johnson seemed as if maybe he not only advocated *legalization,* but also favored *utilization* of a certain recreational substance. And he thought "Aleppo" was a brand of dog food.

Plus I'm not sure what a former moderate Republican and governor of Massachusetts was doing on a Libertarian slate. But Bill Weld does like to have a good time. Maybe running for vice president got him invited to cocktail parties.

Gary Johnson and Bill Weld—the "Toke and Tipple Ticket."

## The End of the World—Thank Goodness

For the last week of the election race I was watching a horror movie starring a leading lady I can't stand and a leading man I detest. So I was rooting for the ghosts, ghouls, and goblins that infest the Haunted (White) House.

However, there were still scenes that made me scream and cover my eyes. (Or my ears, in the case of Trump.) By now I didn't care what happened to either of them. Nonetheless, I was on the edge of my seat waiting to see how the movie would end.

Just when I thought that Donald Trump had been fatally strangled by the tentacles of the Microphone Monster from the *Access Hollywood* crypt, FBI director James Comey was revealed to be one of the undead, leaped out of Anthony Weiner's laptop from hell, and sank his fangs into Hillary's political polls.

I was talking to syndicated newspaper columnist and Fox News commentator Charles Krauthammer just after Clinton's final e-mail scandal broke.

I said, "The secretary of state uses her personal e-mail to send top-secret State Department documents to her weird personal assistant who is married to Anthony Weiner who is so crazy that he's destroyed his political career *twice* by sending lewd Tweets and Instagram photos to random women and who is now under investigation for sexting with an underage girl. And the top-secret State Department documents wind up on *his* computer. How much worse can things get?"

Charles said, "What if the 'underage girl' speaks Russian?"

# 30
# The Revolt
# Against the Elites

The election was terrible because it wasn't an election, it was a rebellion. America is having a civil war, or, to be more accurate, a War of Incivility. The weapons are (mostly) (so far) (except after the election in Portland, Oregon) words. But—goodness!—the words we've heard.

The war is not between Republicans and Democrats or between conservatives and progressives. The war is between the frightened and what they fear. It is being fought by the people who perceive themselves as controlling nothing. They are besieging the people they perceive as controlling everything. We are in the midst of a Perception Insurrection, or, depending on how you perceive it, a Loser Mutiny.

The revolt against the elites targets all manner of preeminence—political elites, business elites, media elites, institutional elites, and, kind reader, you. You're reading a book. What's more, it's a book about a serious subject (however flippantly treated). This marks you as an elite.

You are a member of the in-control faction. You are on the wrong side in the eyes of people screeching "Lock Her Up," but you're also on the wrong side in the eyes of Black Lives Matter protesters, the Tea Party, the Occupy movement, the alt-right, and black-clad anarcho-syndicalist car window smashers—all of whom pride themselves on being out of control.

You are certainly on the wrong side of Bernie Sanders and Donald Trump, even if, by dint of a volte-face between the primary and general elections, you managed to vote for both of them.

Trump is, and Sanders was, the giant inflated balloon face of the revolt. Sanders had a reasonable claim to having no status as an elite, indeed to having no status at all—last of the old New Left cranks, useless appendage in Congress, Vermonter. However, his watery stew of anti-elite Marxism held appeal. And, in fact, it held appeal thanks to elites.

The American ruling class, from Harry Truman through George H. W. Bush, stamped out communism so thoroughly that it now exists only in remote places in comic opera forms. Most Sanders supporters were still DNA molecules the last time a major nation tried to turn the clamorous words of Bernie into calamitous deeds.

Trump, on the other hand, seemed an odd avatar of disestablishmentarianism. But he was oddly right for the job. Donald may be a rich guy, a self-proclaimed member of the 1%, but there's nothing "elite" about him. There's nothing elite about the way he sounds. He sounds like the rest of us. Unfortunately, he sounds like the rest of us after we've had six drinks.

You can imagine playing a round of golf with Trump. (I have it on good authority that he cheats no more than I do.)

Now, imagine a round of golf with Hillary Clinton. She's got twenty Harvard graduate caddies who've read all the golf instruction manuals but who have never been on the links. They spend the whole match telling you— not her—what club to use. The Secret Service is there to make sure you take their suggestion to hit from the fairway with a sand wedge. After you finally make your chip shot the cup and the pin somehow get moved closer to Hillary's lie. ("Lie"—just the word to use in any game involving Hillary.) And the scorecard mysteriously winds up on Hillary's private e-mail server.

Hillary, of course, *is* an elite. She's an elite through educational and institutional sucking-up, an elite by marriage, an elite via carpetbag stowaway trip to the Senate, and an elite courtesy of presidential better-in-the-tent-pissing-out cabinet appointment.

Elites are self-righteous, self-regarding, self-serving, and smug. Hillary is their Queen. But the fact that she snatched the Democratic presidential nomination from Bernie Sanders and garnered more of the popular vote than Donald Trump doesn't mean there isn't a rebellion. It means this kind of internecine warfare brings forth the worst from both sides.

## We Are Not Alone

If it's any comfort, people all over the world are saying, "We're sick of the elites. We're tired of the experts. To hell with the deep thinkers who think they know what we should have better than we do and who—while they're at it—are grabbing everything we've got."

Great Britain's political, business, and trade union leaders were opposed to Brexit. That is, the people who supported the Iraq War plus the people who caused the 2008 global financial crisis plus the people who nationalized the British automobile industry were all in unprecedented agreement on one issue. Voters felt they couldn't go wrong betting against this trifecta.

A similar broad coalition of Colombia's good and great spent five years negotiating a peace treaty with a starving rabble of FARC guerrillas who had been marauding in the country's hinterlands since 1964. A plebiscite was held to ratify the peace agreement, causing voters to tacitly ask, "After fifty-two years of murder, kidnapping, pillage, theft, and trafficking in narcotics, FARC is being offered retirement benefits?" The plebiscite failed.

There can be a reactionary element to the revolt. Such supposedly MSNBC-philic places as Denmark, Sweden, and the Netherlands have seen the rise of nationalist, protectionist, anti-immigration, EU-skeptical political parties. Parties of this kind govern Poland and Hungary.

In France, Marine Le Pen's National Front is now the largest single political party, protesting an influx of foreigners and never mind that the French *are* foreigners.

However, antielitism can come from every political direction. Brazil is in the process of bringing indictments for corruption against practically every one of its politicians—left, right, and middle-of-the-road—for the simple reason that they're guilty of it.

The presidency of Austria was won by a fringe Green candidate who beat a fringe nationalist candidate by a margin so narrow that a do-over had to be scheduled. Candidates from the traditional center-left and center-right Austrian political parties (which have taken turns holding power since the end of WWII) ran fourth and fifth. They came in behind a fringe candidate who was neither fringe Green nor fringe nationalist but just fringe.

Sometimes the antielitism seems to come from never-never land. Among the principle contenders in the 2016 Icelandic parliamentary elections was the "Pirate Party" (symbol: a black sail), featuring a platform plank to give Edward Snowden Icelandic citizenship.

Not to be outdone, citizens of the Philippines gave themselves a dose of electoral homeopathy. Overwhelmed by violent lawbreaking, they elected a violent lawbreaker president. Rodrigo Duterte, former mayor of crime-plagued Davao City, is nicknamed "Duterte Harry."

Even the dull politics of Australia have been in turmoil. Politics in Australia are so dull that the name of the conservative party is the Liberal Party. But Australia has had five prime ministers in six years. Its last election nearly resulted in a hung parliament. A hung parliament! What a tempting idea. Although I suppose hanging legislators is immoral. And it's illegal, except maybe in Queensland if parliamentarians are caught chasing sheep.

In staid Canada they now have a prime minister who's a completely inexperienced dashing young celeb named Justin. I haven't Googled "Canadian politics." (Who would?) But I'm assuming it's Bieber.

## The Populism Pop Quiz

Among poli sci savants, such contrariness at the ballot box is defined as "populism." But, on examination, this is a definition lacking anything definite to explain. At best, it's a name for an opinion common in most democracies: There exists a large herd of the clueless, and running circles around them is a small pack of wiseacres.

Populist opinion has an effect even in political systems where the opinion of the populace doesn't matter. Vladimir Putin harnessed populist outrage at the kleptomaniac incompetents who took possession of Russia after perestroika. Xi Jinping's neo-Maoism makes use of populist anger at the all-the-tea-in-China scale of corruption among the Chinese elites.

There are populist aspects to Islamic terrorism. Fanatical interpretation of "jihad" is antielite. Islamic terrorists hate elites so much that they have suicide squads of elites who go around killing *themselves.*

Countries with strong democratic traditions—and let's hope we live in one—don't harbor the kind of populism that goes psycho, like ISIS. Americans don't appreciate being labeled as clueless, or as wiseacres either. Therefore American politicians rarely take a firm position in favor of populism or against it.

This does not keep our politicians from doing everything they can to provoke the alarums and excursions of populism. The most privileged politicians will give it a try. Hillary Clinton, wiseacre, toiled among clueless Latino, black, and millennial voters in hope of using the alarums of Donald Trump to promote her excursion to the White House.

The results of populism can be disastrous—a Hitler, a Mussolini, a Franco. In Europe, between the First and Second World Wars, the results of populism were more disastrous than the results of anything since the late Middle Ages, when the Black Plague killed a third of the continent's population. At least the Black Plague didn't have popular support.

More often, however, the results of populism are a confused mess—for example, the mess that Andrew Jackson's unwashed supporters left in the White House after his inaugural ball, and the confusion Jackson himself created by vetoing the charter of the Second Bank of the United States, causing the "Panic of 1837" bank run and a collapse in the frontier land speculations of his own supporters.

Blogger alarums and excursions to the contrary, America in 2016 had no Hitler, no Mussolini, no Franco. We didn't even have an Andrew Jackson. (Though Trump promises an immigrant Trail of Tears.) What we had was more like a Perón, and not even the Argentinean dictator Juan, but a mixed-doubles, gender equity pair of Evitas.

*Don't cry for me, mainstream media . . .*

As a method of replacing the sophistry of the wiseacres with the wisdom of the clueless, populism doesn't work. Populism usually doesn't work for the leaders of populist movements, either. The most notable populist in American political history was William Jennings Bryan (1860–1925). His populist appeal was based on an easy fix for the problems of Americans who didn't have much money: Print more.

Bryan ran for president three times on the Democratic ticket, and lost in 1896, 1900, and 1908. Woodrow Wilson appointed him secretary of state. Bryan announced a policy of strict pacifism. The U.S. went to war with Germany anyway. Bryan attempted to gain the Democratic presidential nomination for a fourth time in 1924, and lost. He ended his days making a monkey out of himself at the Scopes trial, defending Tennessee's law against teaching evolution.

The most notable populist in history was Julius Caesar. He—N.B. to those who've been saying the 2016 election "had a sharp edge"—was stabbed to death by twenty-three senators. The conspiracy was a confused mess. Some of the senators ended up stabbing each other. And the political aftermath was so much of a confused mess that it took historian Edward Gibbon 3,589 pages to describe it in *The History of the Decline and Fall of the Roman Empire*.

## Why Are We So Revolting?

The early twenty-first century seems like an odd time to be having a wave of populist rebellions, especially in countries where things are going fairly well—except for the wave of populist rebellions.

We're not in desperate financial straits. The Great Recession of 2008 was painful, with a certain amount of waking up on friends' couches after somebody took the house. But these days practically everyone in America has had a divorce. So we'd been through that before. And if there were any bread lines, they weren't handing out loaves of Love-the-Taste low-carb ThinSlim. America's obesity crisis abides.

We are embroiled in a long war. More than 7,000 American combatants have died during the fifteen years of the War on Terror. But more than 7,800 American combatants died on one day at the Battle of Gettysburg. Streets are not filled with protesters against the war we're in now. Hippies aren't sticking daisies in drones.

We're culturally and politically polarized, but not in a way that would startle an old-school history professor and jolt him awake from his nap in the faculty lounge. The year 1861—*that* was polarized. Fort Sumter isn't taking any incoming.

Yet people are fearful, and they blame their fears on the leadership elite.

Partly this is because the leadership elite hasn't done a very good job. Take the Middle East, for example. Demons have been unleashed in the Middle East. Elites failed to address the problems that caused the demons to be unleashed. Indeed, the elites seem to have been *breeding* demons, in the kennels of elite diplomacy, elite geopolitics, and elite military strategy. Then the elites turned those demons loose in the Middle East as if demons had ever been an endangered species in the region, as if elites were trying to reintroduce them.

One result is murder all over the world. How much farther away from the quarrels and hatreds of the Middle East could a person get than to be at "Latin Night" in a gay nightclub in Orlando, Florida?

Another result is the European refugee crisis. What do the elites care? The refugees aren't crowding the halls and jostling the elites in the corridors of the European Parliament in Brussels. The refugees aren't building shantytowns on the tennis courts at the elites' country clubs.

Young refugee men commit assaults in public places, like the Cologne train station, on public occasions, like New Year's Eve. That's the public's problem. These things don't happen at the *private* dinner parties elites give.

The elites fail and don't suffer any consequences from their failures. As it is with elite carelessness about refugees, so it is with elite carelessness about immigration. To elites immigration means nannies, household staff, and fun new ethnic restaurants. Elites don't see any similarity between Trump's border wall and the gated communities where they live.

To be fair to elites, they've got their problems too. We live in speedy times. Quick changes in social mores, economic norms, and political givens confuse everyone, especially those who thought they were leading The Mores, Norms, and Givens Parade.

We don't have to march in lockstep anymore. People are becoming persons, not masses. This is fun. But difficulties arise after the stride is broken. When the band breaks up it can leave the tubas to be turned into beer bongs; the fellow with the bass drum sitting on the curb playing the solo from "In-A-Gadda-Da-Vida"; the trombonist using his slide to goose the cornet player; and nobody left who can spell "glockenspiel." Meanwhile, the elite drum major is just some dork standing in the middle of the street wearing a goofy hat and waving a stick.

Swift improvements in transport, communication, and technical capacities have combined with a die-off of seventeenth-century import/export thinking (though not an extinction, pax Trump) to produce what is labeled as "globalization." It is a big, worldwide sphere of a word that is the wrong term for the concept of international trade shrinking the Earth to a Pluto-sized planetoid.

We love to have everything from everywhere brought right to our door. Except when we don't. We love going to Yellowstone Park. But do we love having the herds of bison, geysers, trees, mountains, tourists, and bears in our rec room? We'll need to clean the carpet. Then we go to work in the morning and find out a bear ate our job.

The world is a smaller place. Did the elites think this would make everyone get along? Try it with your kids. Put them in a small place, such as the backseat of your car. Now take them to see the world. Take them to, for example, Yellowstone Park from, say, Boca Raton. How are your kids getting along? I guess elites don't take family car trips. I guess elites don't even fly economy class.

Then there's whatever it is that's going on with the Internet. About which I would be the wrong person to ask. I finally got Myspace figured out, only to discover that there was nobody in Myspace except me. But I take it on trust that the "digital revolution" will *change everything* and, for all I know, has done so already. Didn't there used to be a bookstore next to the . . . Hey, where'd Sears go?

I'm glad I can comparison-shop for a refrigerator online and buy any brand that exists and have it delivered the next day with free shipping. But the Kenmore repairman at Sears has now enlisted as a foot soldier in America's opioid addiction attack. How do I get my refrigerator into the FedEx drop box when the icemaker quits working?

Let me say, with the magnificent grasp of the obvious that is professional journalism's hallmark, that all technological advances are disruptive.

For instance, the introduction of the moldboard plow into Europe increased agricultural yield enough to allow for the growth of cities with their manufacturing and trade, thereby diminishing the power of feudal landlords and bringing an end to the Middle Ages. And people were right in the middle of them. Talk about disruptive. Furthermore, I'll bet the reader (not to mention the writer) doesn't have the slightest idea what a "moldboard plow" is. Yet it *changed everything.*

The Industrial Revolution was famously disruptive. The poet William Blake made a plaintive query about the resulting air pollution and poor conditions in the workplace:

*And did the Countenance Divine,*
*Shine forth upon our clouded hills?*
*And was Jerusalem builded here,*
*Among these dark Satanic Mills?*

Of course, this ignores the dark satanic barns people escaped from to go work in the mills. The barns didn't smell very nice either. The Industrial Revolution was a net economic good. But people aren't living large in a world of net economic good. We're living in our own little worlds, often practicing gross economies.

The Digital Revolution is also, I'm told, a net economic good. But it's a good and messy one to an even greater extent than the Industrial Revolution was. Electromagnetic radiation travels at the speed of light. Stationary steam engines traveled at the speed of nothing. When the Industrial Revolution did get moving it was linear. Once you'd seen a railroad train on tracks how surprised could you be by an automobile on pavement? The rails and the roads went somewhere you'd heard of. The Internet, definitionally, is all over the place. And whose bright idea was it to make sure every idiot in the world is in communication with every other idiot?

Therefore all of us idiots, we the people, who make up the populace, which leads to populism, are alarmed by our circumstances and are angry at our leadership elite for not being able to change them.

## Alas, This Is Not a Teachable Moment

The leadership elite doesn't know what to do. And Donald Trump, whether we—or he—like it or not, has just become a member. The conundrum of failure in every revolt against the elites is that when you succeed in overthrowing them you become them. You cease to be a solution and start to be a problem.

A person of libertarian inclinations can understand and sympathize with the revolt against the elites. But what we libertarians have to face is that the revolt is not advancing libertarian values. Populism is not promoting an increase in individual dignity, an increase in individual freedom, or an increase in individual responsibility.

It's doing the opposite—Trump vowing to build a wall between individual dignity and the United States.

To soothe populist discontents politicians have only one piece of equipment—politics. In an attempt to get enough popular support to achieve or retain their elite status, politicians keep making the machinery of politics larger.

It *is* over when the fat lady sings. Politics has become an obese operatic performer, warbling so loudly that none of us bit players can be heard, and so fat that we're shoved into the orchestra pit.

Political power has grown in expense. One-third of the world's GDP is now spent by the politicians in governments. One out of every three things you make is grabbed by governments. If your cat has three kittens, one of them is a government agent.

Political power has grown in scope. Politics casts its net over every little aspect of life. Nothing is so private that it isn't tangled up in politics. In America the latest thing is "transgender bathrooms." We all knew politics were crap. Now we discover that where we take one is a political issue.

When are voters in both political parties going to realize that politics is a two-way street? The politician creates a powerful, huge, heavy, and unstoppable Monster Truck of a government. Then supporters of that politician become shocked and weepy when another politician, whom they detest, gets behind the wheel, turns the truck around, and runs them over.

Make the truck smaller! Yank the engine and install foot pedals. Make it into a Kiddie Kar so that the worst it can do is smack you in the shin.

Populism is a libertarian tragedy. Since the beginning of democracy in fifth-century BC Athens, the greatest danger to democratic institutions has been the demos, the people themselves, the very item that constitutes democracy. Democracy doesn't just contain the seeds of its own destruction, it contains the roots, the fruits, and the whole damn tree.

Each person in a democracy is an individual—the way libertarians say each person is. But when the persons become "the people" and "the people" become "populists," watch out.

What do you think would have happened if that charming old bloke Socrates—lovably eccentric, full of silly questions—had gone around Athens *personally* asking each Athenian, "Should I be condemned to death?"

Individuals would never have killed Socrates. They had to become a mob first.

And what defines a mob? Mobsters. That Cosa Nostra with its code of *omerta* at the Clinton Foundation. Those "Make America Great Again" Crips and Bloods wearing their colors on their baseball caps with brims bumped to the right.

*"I could stand in the middle of Fifth Avenue and shoot somebody and I wouldn't lose voters."*

—Donald Trump, January 23, 2016

We should be learning the value of individual dignity, individual freedom, and individual responsibility from the failure of the elites and the fiasco of their vast political power.

Good things are made by free individuals in free association with other individuals. Notice that that's how we make babies.

Individual freedom is about bringing things together. Politics is about dividing things up.

Elites would have us make babies by putting the woman on this side of the room and the man on that side of the room while the elites stand in the middle taxing sperm and eggs.

But we aren't learning lessons in individual freedom, because we're too scared. We're daunted at the pace of material change, unnerved over social transfigurations, fretful about economic instability, and terrified by terrorism.

Fear is a bad schoolmarm. We've got a monster at the blackboard. How can we learn even 1 + 1 when all we can think is, "EEEEK! Teacher is huge and slimy and has tentacles and two ugly heads!"

So we turn for help to the big, stupid bully at the back of the classroom.

# EPILOGUE

*When the Hell Will This End?*

*Turning the Swamp into a Sewer*

$A$s I write, eight months of the new presidency have gone by. Donald Trump is well into his third trimester. If he's as pregnant with ideas as he says he is he could have one at any moment.

But, as Mrs. Poyser, the worthy farm wife in George Eliot's *Adam Bede*, said, "It's your dead chicks take the longest hatchin'."

Trump has no ideas, not even bad ideas. He has bad instincts, bad impulses, bad information, bad opinions, bad actions, bad values, even bad ideals. But these are all things he has in his hands (with their stubby, pudgy breakfast sausage fingers). There's nothing in his skull. Or, rather, there's nothing in his skull but him. There's no room for anything else. There's so much Trump in Trump's head that it overflows, causing Trump to keep spilling Trump out of Trump's mouth.

Trump had an idea man working for him, an *éminence grise* (or *eminence greasy*) named Steve Bannon. Bannon had lots of ideas. They were very bad ideas. Trump fired him. It wasn't the badness of the ideas that got Bannon fired. It was the *number* of the ideas. They bugged the President. I doubt Trump can tell one idea from another any more than I can tell one bug from another. But when the president found a swarm of indistinguishable creepy-crawly ideations infesting the West Wing he called the exterminator (Gen. John Kelly).

Thus there's no such thing as a "Trumpist" ideology. The *ideo-* is lacking and so is the *-ology*, the "science" or "branch of knowledge" of which the President has not a twig. Trumpism can be explained in 140 characters on Twitter, and Trumpism can *only* be explained in 140 characters on Twitter. Try that with Marxism. QED.

Trump's inchoate ignorance makes smart people angry. It should make them thankful. If he had a clue he'd be really dangerous.

Trump has an ability to harness angry populism. He is a glutton for power, obedience, money, attention, applause, sexual conquest, and (judging by the pouch in his Trump National knit shirt and the sack in his golf slacks) food. If he were something more than a fat ass with the trick of getting a bit into the mouth of a bucking mule . . . If he had a mule wagon that could bear the weight of his ego and his fleshly desires . . . If he knew where he wanted the wagon to go . . .

That is, if Donald Trump had an intellectually coherent ideology he could carry the country straight to hell. As it is, he has to take us on the roundabout route to damnation through twists of error, turns of incompetence, sidetracks of insults and smirking, meanders of lies, rambles of malfeasance, labyrinths of scandal, byways of tactical and strategic idiocy, zig of veiled bigotry, zag of bigotry naked, and the crooked path of being crooked.

Maybe, just maybe, Trump will be kicked out the Oval Office window by America's mulish voters before the nation goes to hell.

If we can make it through 2020 we may survive with democracy intact. Or not.

Given the mindless state of current American political thinking, it wouldn't require much of an intellectually coherent ideology to send the country to perdition. John Birch Society ravings would probably do the trick. "Everything is the fault of the world-wide Communist Conspiracy! There are Communists in North Korea! There are Communists all the way around the world in Cuba! So the Conspiracy is *world-wide*!"

For that matter the Yippie babblings of Abbie Hoffman and Jerry Rubin might work too. "We're so stoned that we have no idea what we're talking about, but if you get as high as we are it will all make sense."

But Donald Trump does not make any sense no matter how blasted you get.


So much for the good news.

But we should be fair to Donald Trump. As the president has said, there are "some very fine people on both sides." No there aren't. There are no courtly southern gentlemen in the Ku Klux Klan. There are no upstanding solid citizen Nazis. Let's get over being fair. Let's give in to loathing Donald Trump. Let's never make any trivial exceptions for any trivial good this trivial man may do. Let's admit to our glee when the man is treated unjustly.

True, if Donald Trump cured cancer the headline in the *New York Times* would read, "Heart Disease Kills More People." Let's revel in it.

It's the most fun we're likely to have with Trump until the next presidential election.

It's no fun making fun of Trump. The best humorists have given it their all trying to make him appear to be more foolish than he is. They've failed. Trump is like his Trump Tower, a hilarious building that looks like a giant bum chromed an accordion and is about to play Lawrence Welk tunes at Fifty-Seventh and Fifth for nickels and dimes. But I can stand on that corner forever making witty quips about Trump Tower's design, ornamentation, and décor, and the building doesn't move.

We're probably not going to impeach Trump. The process is too slow. Impeachment moves at the speed of global warming. And as long as Republicans control Congress the speed of global warming is, officially, zero.

Time will be running short even if Democrats manage to take control of Congress in January 2019. (No sure bet, since Democrats will probably attempt to run Elizabeth Warren and Bernie Sanders for every seat in the House and Senate. And Bernie could be dead by then and might be already.)

Nineteenth-century Republicans began trying to impeach Andrew "some very fine people on both sides" Johnson as soon as Lincoln was assassinated in 1865. They didn't get him to trial before the Senate until 1868.

Arrests for the Watergate break-in were made in June 1972, just months after Nixon's second inauguration. Impeachment proceedings weren't begun against him until July 1974. He didn't resign until August. It took two years and two months before the helicopter "muckevac" of Nixon from the White House.

The attempt to impeach Bill Clinton lasted almost four-and-a-half years. Ken Starr started his wide-ranging "Redneck Riviera" Whitewater investigation in August 1994, finally turning up evidence of presidential oral sex in January 1998, which in February 1999 the Senate found—if you'll pardon the expression—hard to swallow.

The most likely grounds for turning Trump out of office would be, I suppose, the "Russia Scandal." But the administration's collusion with Russia lacks pretty faces (Donald Trump Jr. excepted) or random violence or other clickbait. When something doesn't get on YouTube it simply doesn't make an impression on the American public these days.

The firing of Michael Flynn, for instance. Imagine if fifty-five years ago JFK's National Security Advisor Mc-George Bundy had been caught playing footsie with the Soviet ambassador to the U.S. Anatoly Dobrynin in the middle of the Cuban Missile Crisis. Then, further imagine, that after President Kennedy fired Bundy, Kennedy himself invited Dobrynin and Soviet Foreign Minister Andrei Gromyko to the White House and spilled the beans to them about highly classified U.S. intelligence operations.

It would have caused quite a hullabaloo, and World War III.

But the 1962 Cuban Missile Crisis was back when history was still in its first, tragic iteration and had yet to repeat itself as farce.

That was Khrushchev, "We will bury you" vs. Kennedy, "We shall pay any price, bear any burden, meet any hardship, invade any Vietnam . . ."

This is Putin, "We will troll you" vs. Trump, "We'll call room service."

That was the CIA vs. the KGB. This is "Get Smart" vs. Dr. Evil's younger, dumber brother Professor Awful.

Khrushchev wanted to dominate the globe. Putin snatched Crimea, a beach resort. "We will bury you—in the sand."

Kennedy wanted to save the nation. "Ask not what your country can do for you . . . " Trump wants to brand it. "Ask for the room service hamburger well-done."

Under the tremendous, huge leadership of President Trump and his very, very good, really great advisors such as Hulk Hogan, Gene Simmons, Bobby Knight, Ted Nugent, Mike Tyson, Kid Rock, Lou Ferrigno, Dennis Rodman, Wayne Newton, and Gary Busey, lots of really very incredible enormous things are getting done.

The Republicans wrote a healthcare bill that was more complicated, expensive, unsustainable, and stupid than Obamacare. Some said it was an impossible task. And the Republicans would have passed the bill, too, if it hadn't been National Alzheimer's Awareness Week with a number of Republican congressmen raising awareness of Alzheimer's by forgetting to vote "yea."

America launched fifty-nine Tomahawk cruise missiles at Syria and everything has been quiet in the Middle East since then.

Neil Gorsuch was appointed to the Supreme Court after it was patiently explained (twice) to President Trump that he couldn't nominate Antonin Scalia because Scalia was very, very, really tremendously dead.

Homeland Security is busy everywhere expelling illegal immigrants including the so-called "Dreamers" who thought they could stay in America just because they'd been here all their lives and were American. Well, "Dream On," kids. (In case you were wondering why the paperboy was snatched off your front porch and thrown into a black van by ICE agents wearing body armor.)

FBI director James Comey got fired. "For the same reasons Ike fired J. Edgar Hoover," said White House Press Secretary Sarah Huckabee Sanders in a quote I just made up because I'm a member of the "failing media" printing "fake news." (But it does sound like something she'd say.)

Tax reform will be so, so great, so spectacular. Just you wait. And wait. And wait. And wait. And wait.

The U.S. announced its withdrawal from the Paris climate accord because of something on the order of "The climate in Paris is lousy. I've been to Paris. In the winter when it drizzles. In the summer when it sizzles. That's for losers."

The Keystone XL pipeline was approved. Concerns about oil spills on Native American tribal lands were addressed in a positive manner. "Any oil that spills on Indian reservations, the Indians get to keep it. It's theirs for free," some Trump appointee at the Department of the Interior said according to more fake news you're reading here in the "lame-stream" press.

Meanwhile executive orders have been signed defining pollution as "something poor people do." Trump knows a lot of rich people. He finds them to be really, really clean, very remarkably clean. They don't smell at all. Except for a whiff of Donald Trump Success After Shave or Ivanka Trump Eau de Parfum on the gals.

Speaking of what stinks, Trump retains the support of about one-third of American voters. And, although I'd love to blame this on Trump, he seems to be doing everything he can—including becoming besties with Chuck Schumer and Nancy Pelosi—to get rid of his supporters. So it must be somebody else's fault. Maybe mine. I've been ranting for years about how infuriating, confusing, and disappointing the federal government is. It's possible that someone took me seriously. I've never had it happen before. But, if so, I'm sorry. I'm a humorist. You're supposed to laugh at me, not listen.

Anyway, Trump supporters are much more infuriated, confused, and disappointed by the federal government than I am. I think it's funny and always has been and always will be. They do not think it's funny. Although I do have to admit that Trump supporters are showing a fine sense of irony in the way they're expressing their wrath. They're using the federal government to punish the federal government.

Of course Trump supporters don't mind Trump. Literally they don't "mind" him. They don't pay very much attention to him at all. Trump's just signage, a signal of anger, confusion, and disappointment. Trump is the little silhouette on the door to the anti-government men's room. If you're so mad at the federal government that you use the government's postal service to mail the government a turd, are you disappointed when it's delivered?

# GLOSSARY

*Punditese—English*

The 2016 election cycle has been subject to extensive commentary by political pundits such as myself. But what we pundits are saying isn't always clear to a general audience.

This is because political pundits speak a foreign language, Punditese.

It can be difficult to translate Punditese into English. For example, the word "gaff." As detailed in Chapter 9, pundits described Vice President Biden as a person who made "gaffs." But there is no precise English equivalent for "gaff."

When a pundit says a candidate made a gaff, the pundit may mean the candidate has said something most pundits believe but do not care to publicly state (e.g., "Basket of deplorables"). Or the pundit may mean the candidate doesn't realize that not everything that comes into the candidate's mind has to come out of his mouth (e.g., "Miss Universe is getting fat"). Or the pundit simply may be pointing out that the candidate has said what is so. (The last being a difficult concept to express in Punditese.)

*There are also two distinct dialects of Punditese—
Conservative Punditese (CP) and Liberal Punditese (LP). Like
English and English with a thick, drunken Irish brogue, they
are closely related linguistically but often mutually unintelligible. There was a third dialect, Objective Punditese (OP),
but it is extinct. The last two native speakers of OP, Michael
Oakeshott and Isaiah Berlin, died in the 1990s.*

## Punditese Words and Phrases
## with Their Meanings Given in English

**political cycle**—what a pundit calls an election because "political cycle" sounds more highfalutin, as if the pundit's been
reading Oswald Spengler's *Decline of the West* instead of USA-
TODAY.com.

**front-runner**—a candidate whose name is familiar to people
whose lives are so empty that a call, text, or website pop-up
from a political pollster is the highlight of their day.

**strong contender**—maybe they've also heard this candidate's
name.

**plausible contender**—the pundit knows all about this candidate; that's how empty the pundit's life is.

**possible contender**—candidate did something Jimmy Fallon
mentioned in his monologue last night.

**candidate is closing the gap in the polls**—Jimmy Fallon
showed a video clip of it.

**dark horse candidate**—hopeless candidate pundit is talking
about.

**hopeless candidate**—dark horse candidate other pundits are
talking about.

**inside the Beltway**—I, the pundit, am so well-informed and savvy about Washington that I know that when you're driving south from New York on I-95 the interstate forks in Maryland, with I-95 going left, clockwise around the District of Columbia, and I-495 going right, counterclockwise around the District of Columbia, until the two roads rejoin in Virginia, forming a ring or "beltway" around our nation's capital.

**Beltway insider**—me.

**Beltway insiders**—me and a couple of low-level congressional staffers with whom I had drinks.

**reliable source**—me.

**inside source**—me.

**inside sources**—me and one of the low-level congressional staffers.

**reliable sources** (CP)—me and Matt Drudge.

**reliable sources** (LP)—me and the members of my Georgetown power yoga class.

**wise men** (unironic)—the pundit speaking of himself or herself in the third-person plural.

**wise men** (ironic)—other pundits, and they're wrong.

**hinge point**—the 2016 election cycle will be very different from now on in a way that will look to you, the uninitiated, as if things are the same. But I, the pundit, will be here to explain how different things are, compared with the way they were before I explained them to you.

**game changer**—like a hinge point but so obvious that there's nothing for the pundit to explain and the pundit has to say, "That's a real game changer," over and over again.

**tip of the iceberg**—I, the pundit, am trying to attract attention to myself by alarming you about a thing. The alarming thing is as obvious as a game changer, but I have special knowledge, unavailable to any of the candidates or the captain of the *Titanic*, that seven eighths of this alarming thing is hidden or concealed.

**double down**—candidate making the same mistake twice.

**as I have said before**—pundit making the same mistake twice.

**exit strategy**—as Abbie Hoffman called it, "Yelling 'Theater!' in a crowded fire."

**spin**—what you're hearing from the pundit, not that the pundit realizes it.

**fiscally conservative and socially liberal** (LP)—Republican about whom I can't think of anything truly damning to say, but give me a minute.

**fiscally conservative and socially liberal** (CP)—Republican who couldn't be trusted to oppose Gloria Allred's appointment to the Supreme Court.

**women's health** (LP)—abortion.

**hard-liner** (LP)—any Republican to the right of Nelson Rockefeller, e.g., Ronald Reagan.

**far right** (LP)—any Republican to the right of Nelson Rockefeller and not, e.g., Reagan, dead yet.

**far left** (LP)—doesn't exist.

**far left** (CP)—the inspirational quotes on Starbucks coffee cups, and the list goes on from there.

**big money**—money that has not been offered to the pundit.

**dark money**—nobody has offered the pundit *any* money.

**political analysts say**—some other journalist told me.

**political analysts agree**—two other journalists told me.

**highly placed source**—anyone dumb enough to answer my e-mails or phone calls.

**highly placed source speaking on condition of anonymity because . . .** —because he or she is dumb but not suicidal.

**on background**—the highly placed source is pulling this out of his ass.

**on deep background**—the highly placed source is pulling this out of somebody else's ass.

**studies show**—I'm pulling this out of my own ass.

**any sentence beginning with To be accurate, The facts are, or Careful research shows**—I Googled it.

**balanced assessment**—what I'm saying.

**impartial assessment**—what I said already, and now I'm saying again.

**a voice of reason**—someone who agrees with me, such as, for example, me.

**Democratic insiders** (CP)—the *New York Times*.

**Democratic insiders** (LP)—the *New York Times*.

**Republican insiders** (LP)—Rush Limbaugh.

**Republican insiders** (CP)—Rush Limbaugh.

**Beltway veteran**—liar.

**seasoned Beltway veteran**—liar, thief, and cheat.

**Beltway bandit, syn. highly paid lobbyist** (use of noun "lobbyist" w/o modifier "highly paid" is unidiomatic)—seasoned Beltway veteran who is presumed to have confessed to lying, thieving, and cheating by registering as a lobbyist.
(LP)—lobbyist for businesses, industries, or trade associations.

(CP)—lobbyist for labor unions, environmental organizations, or nonprofits other than the NRA.

**partisan**—they're wrong.

**nonpartisan**—I'm right.

**conservative stalwart** (CP)—a Koch brother.

**conservative stalwarts** (LP)—both Koch brothers.

**liberal stalwart** (CP)—anyone to the left of David Brooks, including David Brooks.

**liberal stalwart** (LP)—David Brooks, in his heart of hearts.

**traditional media**—the newspaper that fired me.

**mainstream media**, also **lamestream media** (CP)—bootlicking, ass-kissing, pinko milksops.

**right-wing talk radio and Fox News** (LP)—the voices people hear when they aren't taking their meds.

**speaking truth to power**—in my dreams that's what I do, although, even in my dreams, I'm careful to do it from a safe distance. Kim Jong Un, you stink.

**food insecurity** (LP)—hunger in America, never mind the high rate of obesity among America's poor. (An example of "synonymic refactualization," a linguistic feature of Punditese in which the pundit proffers a statistical analysis that the public doubts or ignores, and the statistical analysis is proved by giving it a new name.)

**climate change** (LP)—weather.

**politics**—politicians lying.

**insider politics**—politicians lying to each other.

**politics as usual**—politics.

**grassroots politics**—the candidate has attracted an impressive number of clueless people with nothing better to do than randomly phone other people at dinnertime.

**dog whistle politics** (LP)—a Republican candidate makes a seemingly innocuous statement that his (DWP is practiced only by GOP males) supporters—and only his supporters—correctly hear as racist, sexist, homophobic, and insensitive while his opponents remain clueless. But the pundit, thanks to his superpowers as a political analyst, is . . .

*There's no need to fear,*
*Underdog is here!*

. . . able to detect the racism, sexism, homophobia, and insensitivity.

**retail politics**—candidates lying to members of the electorate one by one.

**effective media campaign**—candidates lying to members of the electorate all at the same time.

**earned media**—see Jimmy Fallon, above.

**effective social media campaign**—someone on candidate's campaign staff, probably a nineteen-year-old volunteer, knows what Reddit is.

**is a Washington insider**—candidate knows where the bones are buried.

**is not a Washington insider**—candidate who will dig up the whole yard.

**passionate advocate of**—candidate is having a manic episode.

**passionate opponent of**—friends say candidate needs rest.

**claims his/her remarks were taken out of context**—gotcha!

**in fairness to**—here comes a great big bitch slap of a backhanded compliment.

**out of touch with ordinary Americans** (LP)—candidate doesn't even try to pretend to be stupid, broke, and dressed in sweatpants from Walmart.

**out of touch with ordinary Americans** (CP)—candidate favors immigration reform because he/she can't get the leaf blower started and supports legalization of gay marriage and preservation of abortion rights because his/her son/daughter is a horn-dog/slut.

**X expresses 100 percent support for Y**—Y feels point of X's short, sharp cutting instrument between shoulder blades.

**X expresses 200 percent support for Y**—X has told Y, "I know where your children go to school."

**loyal Democrat** (CP)—as was Mary Jo Kopechne.

**loyal Republican** (LP)—in an irreversible coma.

**appealing to the Republican base** (LP)—wearing a bedsheet with eyeholes to a protest at an abortion clinic while carrying an assault rifle and holding hands with Jesus.

**alt-right** (LP)—and at home in his bedroom there's a shrine to Timothy McVeigh.

**appealing to the Democratic base** (CP)—chasing someone off campus for failing to give a trigger warning in a safe space after looting a liquor store to demonstrate that police are implicitly racist.

**major Republican Party donors** (LP)—the Koch brothers, Attila the Hun, Dr. Evil, the Penguin, Lucrezia Borgia, Goldfinger, Witch-King of Angmar, and the Koch brothers.

**major Democratic Party donors** (CP)—Edward Snowden, Ayatollah Khamenei, Bashar al-Assad, Abu Bakr al-Baghdadi,

Raúl Castro, Planned Parenthood, the UN, everyone in the entertainment industry who ever wants to work again, and Bernie Madoff.

**waste, fraud, and abuse** (CP)—government.

**increasing government efficiency** (LP and CP)—monkeys may fly out of my butt.

**reinventing government** (LP)—making a patent application for a circular object capable of rolling back and forth.

**term limits, entitlement reform, privatization of Social Security** (CP)—unicorns, flying ponies, and candy-flavored rainbows.

**raising awareness of** (LP)—won't shut up about.

**social justice** (LP)—increasing minimum wage to $40/hour and requiring grade school students to read Ta-Nehisi Coates.

**Donald Trump**—candidate all pundits, liberal or conservative, can be counted on to deplore because every time he says anything, even "Hello," he attracts more attention than any political pundit has attracted since Saint Peter was communications director and Christ was campaigning.

**Donald Trump** (LP)—the true face of the GOP.

**Donald Trump** (CP)—democracy is government by the people and 50 percent of people are below average in intelligence, mathematical fact.

"Perhaps in that flight of birds . . . the leader was not really a bold spirit trusting to its own initiative and hypnotizing the flock to follow it in its deliberate gyrations. Perhaps the leader was the blindest, the most dependent of the swarm, pecked into taking wing before the others, and then pressed and chased and driven by a thousand hissing cries and fierce glances whipping it on."

—George Santayana,
*The Last Puritan*

# ACKNOWLEDGMENTS

Sometime early in 2016 I was at a cocktail party with my editor and publisher Morgan Entrekin who, for his sins, has commissioned every book I've published. I said to him, in a mood of slightly drunken self-pity and guilt, "I haven't gotten much done on what you've paid me an advance for—because, damn it, I've ended up scribbling and yakking so much about this election."

"Oh, what the hell," said Morgan, "let's turn *that* into a book."

Thus this compendium of scribble and yak. Various elements of the book—now rather hopelessly jumbled together—originally appeared in the *Daily Beast*, the *Stansberry Digest*, the *Weekly Standard*, *Esquire*, *Briefings*, and BBC radio scripts or were heard in speeches I've given or commentaries I've done.

Knowing that the sum of the parts may be greater than the whole, I give heartfelt thanks to John Avlon and Will Rahn at the *Daily Beast*, Porter Stansberry and Carli Flippen at the *Stansberry Digest*, Richard Starr at the *Weekly Standard*, Jay Fielden and Mark Warren at *Esquire*, Glenn Rifkin and the late Joel Kurtzman at *Briefings*, Richard Vadon and Barney Rowntree at the BBC, Carl Bernstein with whom I teamed in a number of appearances titled "A Funny Thing Happened on the Way to the White House," Don Epstein and David Buchalter at my lecture agency Greater Talent Network, host Peter Sagal and my fellow panelists on the NPR program *Wait . . . Wait . . . Don't Tell Me . . .* , Ed Crane and Peter Goettler at the Cato Institute, Joseph Bast at the Heartland Institute, and Greg Lindsay at the Centre for Independent Studies in Australia.

To take my muddling through a mess of an election and get the results set into type and sent to the printer would have been impossible without the heroic efforts of Grove Atlantic Assistant Editor Allison Malecha. May she be blessed with a long life so wonderful that she never sees (or has to edit a book about) an election like this again.

Further enormous gratitude to Managing Editor Julia Berner-Tobin, Copyeditor Susan Gamer, Production Director Sal Destro, Publicity Manager Justina Batchelor, Publicity Director Deb Seager, and Art Director Gretchen Mergenthaler who designed the splendid cover that is graced by the brilliant illustrations of the artist who goes by the name DonkeyHotey.

And thank you Tina O'Rourke. As a result of you paying attention to what really mattered during the Electoral Dark Ages, the house hasn't fallen down, the cars aren't up on blocks, the dogs haven't run off, and the children and their father are not starved to death.

# ABOUT THE AUTHOR

P. J. O'Rourke has written eighteen books on subjects as diverse as politics and cars and etiquette and economics. *Parliament of Whores* and *Give War a Chance* both reached #1 on the *New York Times* bestseller list. He is a contributing editor at the *Weekly Standard*, H. L. Mencken Research Fellow at the Cato Institute, a regular panelist on NPR's *Wait Wait . . . Don't Tell Me*, and editor-in-chief of the web magazine *American Consequences*. He lives in rural New England, as far away from the things he writes about as he can get.